...OR NOT
TO BE

A Collection of Suicide Notes

...OR NOT TO BE

A Collection of Suicide Notes

Marc Etkind

Riverhead Books, New York

Riverhead Books
Published by The Berkley Publishing Group
200 Madison Avenue
New York, New York 10016

Care has been taken to trace the ownership and obtain permission, if necessary, for
excerpts from the works of others. If any errors have occurred, they will be corrected
in subsequent printings provided notification is sent to the publisher. Certain names have
been changed to protect the privacy of some individuals.

First Riverhead trade paperback edition: February 1997

The Putnam Berkley World Wide Web site address is http://www.berkley.com/berkley

Library of Congress Cataloging-in-Publication Data
   —Or not to be : a collection of suicide notes / Marc Etkind.
      p.   cm.
     ISBN 1-57322-580-0
     1. Suicide—Psychological aspects.   I. Etkind, Marc.
   HV6545.072 1997
   616.85'8445—dc20   96-28863
                                            CIP

Printed in the United States of America

10 9 8 7 6 5 4

Contents

Introduction   vii

1. The Birth of the Suicide Note   1

2. Love and Hate   6

3. To the Point?   12

4. Disgrace   16

5. Altruistic Suicide   27

6. The Artistic Temperament   35

7. In Public   56

8. Hollywood Endings   66

9. Suicide Diaries   71

10. Mass Suicide   82

11. Around the World   87

12. The Right to Die   100

Acknowledgments   109

Introduction

"I have never read a suicide note that I would want to have written."
—Edwin Shneidman, suicide expert

This book of suicide notes is pornography. In reading these, the most intimate documents, you are a sadistic voyeur, transforming someone else's pain into your own pleasure. Suicide notes simply should not be read by strangers.

A book of suicide notes creates this gut reaction. It seems wrong to make public someone's private pain. But this assumes that all suicide notes are meant to be private. It was no coincidence that the rise in suicide notes corresponded with the rise of newspapers in the eighteenth century. Suicide notes only became common when there was an outlet for them to be read. Ever since, suicides have been making their notes public: The Japanese writer Yukio Mishima gathered a crowd to hear his final speech; artist Ralph Barton mailed his suicide note to *The New York Times*; and now there is even a site on the Internet where writers post their suicide notes for comment and review. In fact, every note in this book has been previously published. Many of the notes were written to advance some cause: Vietnam war protestors' notes proclaim a hope for peace; assisted suicide notes advocate the right to die; and artists craft their notes as the final piece in their portfolio. Instead of being intensely personal documents, many suicide notes should be read as social acts. They are the last desperate attempts at communication with the wider world.

If suicide notes are indeed attempts at communication, then they are dismal failures. We all hope that as we near death, we'll have a moment of understanding, where our thoughts crystallize and we can sum up our existence with eloquence. But if the suicide attempter had this moment of understanding, he probably wouldn't kill himself. And there lies the ultimate paradox of the suicide note: If someone could think clearly enough to leave a cogent note, that person would probably be able to recognize that suicide was a bad idea. Or as Edwin

Shneidman writes, "In order to commit suicide, one cannot write a meaningful note; conversely, if one could write a meaningful note, one would not have to commit suicide."

Suicide notes, written when people are at their psychological worst, are anything but the voice of clarity. Instead they are bizarre, rambling, angry and above all, sad documents of disturbed minds. Since each note offers a distorted view, it is only by looking at the entire collection that we begin to see coherence. And it is that search for coherence that is the real justification for a study of suicide notes. With suicide now claiming more lives than murder, shouldn't we try to gain insight into the suicidal mind? The study of suicide notes, written at that key moment when the mind decides to die, may offer an understanding.

The suicidal mind is indeed revealed in the notes. Many notes show a distorted logic that twists every incident and detail to fit the answer of suicide. The logic is often reinforced with absolute words like "never" and "only" showing that the writer can see only one solution. The notes are often jammed with petty details—funeral arrangements, shopping lists, reminders to buy birthday presents. It's as if the writer is using his focus on the little things to distract his mind away from the larger thought—that he is actually about to take his life. In the end what is most striking about the notes is their remarkable similarity. Whether written by men or women, Americans or foreigners, in this century or last, the notes show that the psychological state needed to commit suicide varies little; there are only so many ways to express extreme pain.

The study of the notes will provide insight into suicide but it won't offer the answer to one puzzle: why so few suicides, less than one in five, actually write a note. Psychologists have analyzed many variables, including age, sex, and class, they can't find any difference between those who leave notes and those who don't. Perhaps some just feel their act says it all. Or perhaps suicide scientist Erwin Stengel has found the reason: "Whether the writers of suicide notes differ in their attitudes from those who leave no notes behind it is impossible to say. Possibly, they differ from the majority only in being good correspondents."

The following collection will allow the reader to decide just how good a correspondent the suicide note-writer really is.

...OR NOT TO BE

A Collection of Suicide Notes

1

The Birth of the Suicide Note

You need not expect to see me back again, for I have made
up my mind to make away with—Margaret Moyes

This was the note left by 23-year-old Margaret Moyes. On September 11, 1838, she paid her sixpence, climbed to the top of the London Monument, and jumped to her death. Moyes's suicide attracted tremendous public attention. In the countless newspaper articles that followed, readers were forced to question the prevailing attitudes and laws punishing suicide: was Moyes really a criminal or a suffering soul?

In the Hollywood view of the world, it's hard to imagine a suicide without a note, but prior to the eighteenth century very few people bothered to spend their last tormented moments writing down their thoughts. Few people knew how to read or write, and even if they could, the last thing they would want to do would be to broadcast their suicide to the world, for they would be demonized, their body dragged through town and staked at a crossroads, and their family's property and possessions confiscated.

But in the eighteenth century, with a dramatic increase in literacy, a few eccentric souls decided they would attempt communication, even if it meant eternal damnation. At the same time, newspapers catering to the growing masses of the newly literate decided to publish these last-moment messages. When the public failed to show outrage and, in fact, showed great eagerness to read these documents, a new phenomenon was born: the strange combination of literacy and lunacy we call the suicide note.

The role that the press played in the promotion of suicide notes cannot be underestimated. As Michael MacDonald and Terence Murphy argue in their book *Sleepless Souls*, newspapers gave potential suicides, for the first time in history, access to a mass audience. The suicide using the note could now craft his death to achieve sympathy, revenge, or posterity. Suicide was now self-expression.

By printing suicide notes, the newspapers even taught the potential suicide how to craft his message. As *Sleepless Souls* states, "They [the newspapers] printed suicide notes whose conventions and rhetoric taught those who were about to die how to address the audience they were about to leave." In short, newspapers helped decide the tone, form, and language of a suicide note.

Through these notes, the attitude toward suicide changed. Once suicides were considered satanic, now the notes showed them to be human, suffering from such common problems as poverty, infidelity, and plain bad luck. The messages seemed to say that, if not for circumstance, everyone was perilously close to suicide. As the public began to identify with the victims and their families, the laws punishing self-murder relaxed, and the suicide was treated with sympathy, not scorn.

All this took place on the public stage of the newspaper. Ultimately, the advent of suicide notes established the act as a public phenomenon. No longer the solitary act of madmen, the suicide wanted his act publicized, for the note was written to be read.

To any good Christian to whom this may come.

Courteous Reader,

To whom this melancholy Affair may be made known, be not too censorious before you have thoroughly survey'd the Cause of my Misfortune: Therefore look on my Condition with Compassion, and not Ridicule, and believe me to be of honest Parents, who bestowed on me Some education, whereby I have carried a fair Character; and, I bless my God, honest to all men; but of a Sudden deprived of Thought and Reason, am become odious to myself, and of Course

despicable to my Friends and Acquaintance, and as such am un-
worthy of any longer being upon Earth; yet thro' the Merits of my
Blessed Saviour, I hope for Salvation, and when this unworthy Body
is laid waste, my Soul may Still remain among the Blessed, for, to the
utmost of my Knowledge, I have wronged no body. . . .

From the suicide note of Lewis Kennedy, the gardener to the Duke of
Bedford. Kennedy slit his throat in 1743.

It is easy to see how the publication of Kennedy's moving note might
soften public opinion about suicide. Yet, at the same time, Kennedy deliberately crafted his note to have this effect, for if his family faced the full
punishment for his act, they would be financially ruined. These early notes
have a fascinating dynamic: with the ulterior motive of avoiding punishment, it is difficult to know what is genuine and what is crafted.

My Dear,

This is to acquaint you, that you are the fatal cause of this ac-
tion; your behavior to me has drove me distracted. We might have
lived happily and in credit, had your conduct been like mine. I hope
the man who has been the cause of it, will think of this sad catastro-
phe. My child I have left behind I commend to God's care, and I pray
God forgive you; and, as I am weary of life, hope he will forgive me,
your husband, John Stracey

Stracey hung himself in 1750.

This note of hate, meant to inflict lasting guilt on the survivors, was
found in his pocket.

Filled with hate, disgrace, and self-blame, notes from centuries ago are remarkably contemporary. It's as if the industrial revolution, the rise and fall
of Communism, and the atomic bomb had no influence on the psyche.

No psychologist has done a formal comparison of eighteenth- and
twentieth-century notes, but psychologist Antoon Leenaars has con-

ducted a rigorous test of a sample from 1945 and 1985. These forty years have seen the birth of the computer and the turmoil of the sixties, as well as other major changes. But Leenaars was unable to find major differences in the notes. "We can conclude that over the past 40 years, the psychological state of the suicide—a human malaise—has been relatively constant. . . . The 'reasons' for suicide have been generally the same. There have not been many differences in 'I love you,' 'I am in pain,' 'I am sick,' 'This is the only thing I can do.' "

It is likely that a study of earlier notes will generate the same findings. Although suicide notes may have been a new phenomenon for the eighteenth century, they seem to record fundamental symptoms and universal conditions.

Dear wife, before this reaches you I shall be no more: The weight of my misfortunes, which I have brought upon myself by my criminal intercourse with Mrs. D. I am not able to bear any longer, and am therefore determined to quit a life, that for some years has been but of little use to you or my children. Farewell, for ever. From him who was once an indulgent husband.

This man hung himself in 1770.

Good bye my dear dear little wife. I hope you will soon get a kind and more prosperous if not independent husband for you are worthy of it . . . I tried every move but without success to put myself beyond debt and difficulty and live in an independcy [sic] with the world but you have only to be branded with the name of Dewing and its the guinea stamp to be poor and in difficulties however vigilant, persevering industrious & economising you may be. My father grandfathers uncle aunts sisters brothers cousins & c that bear the fated name I hope I leave no offspring behind to inherit it, to be look [sic] upon coldly by the world to be shunned and frowned at by acquain-

*tance and treated with a contumely and contempt by those you love
and respect all because you are poor and fates against you.*

This excerpt is from the note left by George Dewing, a bankrupt printer who committed suicide in 1861. Dewing's poverty may have been an important factor in his death, but he died hating the world, his family, his name, and himself.

Both the Old and New Testaments include accounts of suicide, but the Bible never once condemns the act. In fact, early Christianity actually encouraged suicide by rewarding martyrs with a quick trip to heaven. Only in the fifth century, with the writing of Saint Augustine, did suicide become a sin. He reasoned that life is a gift from God and to reject that gift is to reject God.

Fear of God (as well as the harsh punishment to the victim's body and his family) no doubt prevented many suicides. But these three notes, all written in the nineteenth century, show a progression of God's grip weakening.

My God, O my God, pray forgive me and take care of my dear wife.
From an old house painter

*In hopes the Almighty will pardon me; was I sure of that, I should
leave the world without the least regret.*
A sixty-four-year-old seamstress

*From the agony I have been through for no reason whatever I can
only come to the logical conclusion that if there is a god that he is
not so good as is made out.*
A young clerk

2

Love and Hate

It is said that London police can always distinguish among corpses fished out of the Thames, between those who drowned themselves because of unhappy love affairs and those drowned for debt. The fingers of the lovers are almost invariably lacerated by their attempts to save themselves by clinging to the piers of bridges. In contrast, the debtors apparently go down like slabs of concrete, without struggle and without afterthought.

—A. Alvarez

Love

Love may be the most frequent word in suicide notes. Perhaps *love*'s popularity lies in the fact that it can take on so many meanings.

> *My Darling, To love you as I do and live without you is more than I can bear. I love you so completely, wholeheartedly without restraint. I worship you, that is my fault . . . Without you life is unbearable. This is the best way. This will solve all our problems . . . If it is possible to love in the hereafter, I will love you even after death. God have mercy on both our souls. He alone knows my heartache and love for you.*

This note was left by a thirty-five-year-old. With the line "God have mercy on both our souls," the writer implicates an ex-lover as the cause of the suicide.

My dear sister, we are both going blissfully into the uncertain Beyond. Please think of me once in a while and marry only for love! I couldn't do that and, since I couldn't resist love, I'm going with him.

Baroness Mary Vetsera committed suicide with the love of her life, the heir to the Austro-Hungarian throne, Archduke Rudolf. While the two would have preferred to marry, Rudolf had both a wife and a strong Catholic faith that made divorce out of the question. One of the ironies of the suicidal mind is that it can make the sin of double suicide seem more acceptable than the sin of divorce.

Dear, It will soon be all now over. My last word to you is the same that I have said during all these long, sad years—love.

The note Karl Marx's daughter Eleanor left to her lover, Edward Aveling. While involved with Marx, Aveling had numerous affairs and even secretly married another woman. There is speculation that the pair formed a suicide pact, but Aveling didn't live up to his end of the bargain. He did however, provide Eleanor with the poison she used to kill herself.

Psychologist Edwin Shneidman has pointed out the ambiguity of the word *love* in Marx's note. Here it can mean bitterness, regret, disappointment, tenderness, nostalgia, helplessness—or all of the above.

I'll kill myself tomorrow, unable to stand existence without the woman who had been my sole joy, the only happiness in my life. For the last two and a half months I have struggled; today I am at the edge. I don't have much hope to see her again, but who knows? At least I am plunging into the void where one no longer suffers. I wish to be buried (this is my formal wish) in the tomb that I have had built in the Ixelles cemetery for my dear Marguerite, the vault which I own. My body should be placed in the central resting place just above her. And never, for any reason, must I be placed in the highest chamber. I ask that her portrait and a lock of her hair, which I will have on me when I die, be placed in my coffin, which should be as similar as possible to that of my dearest Marguerite's. On the tombstone, below my dearest Marguerite's inscription, in the same characters and the same style of writing, write these words: "Georges, 29th of April, 1837 - 30th of September, 1891: ai—je bien pu vivre deux mois et demi sans toi?"

From the note left by General Boulanger. Boulanger was on the verge of becoming the dictator of France, but instead relinquished his power to devote himself to his dying lover, Marguerite. Two months after her death, Boulanger went to her grave site and shot himself.

A portrait of Marguerite was found with Boulanger's body. It was underneath his shirt, stuck to his chest with dried blood. The final line of Boulanger's note translates: "Can I really have lived two and a half months without you?"

Hate

"No one kills himself except as he wishes the death of another."

—William Stekel

These suicide notes, stoked with hate, certainly prove Stekel's point. While the lethal wound may affect only the victim, the note is meant to inflict lasting pain and guilt on the survivor.

Dear Betty:
I hate you.
Love,
George

This brief suicide note explains so much.

I wish to be buried in Uniondale Cemetery No 4, facing Marshall Ave., so that I may be able to see the fair-weather friends and thank them for their sarcastic and hateful remarks.

From a hate-filled suicide note.

I present this picture of another woman—the girl I thought I married. May you always remember I loved you once but died hating you.

A man wrote this note on the back of his wife's photograph. She had recently run away with his brother.

Often it is not just the note, but the way someone chooses to kill himself that is meant to hurt someone else:

- A mother who disapproved of her daughter's fiancé killed herself at the wedding reception.
- A California woman lay across the tracks of the commuter train on which her husband was riding.
- A thirty-year-old New York man, depressed over his breakup with his girlfriend, blew himself up on her doorstep.
- A man wrapped himself in dynamite, wired it to a light switch, and connected the switch to the front door. When his wife opened the door . . .

To whom it may concern: Goodbye you old prick and when I mean prick you are a prick. Hope you fall with the rest of us, you yellow bastard. May the precinct get along without you.

From a note written by a thirty-seven-year-old cop. He waited in a bar to kill his sergeant. When the sergeant didn't show up, he shot himself instead.

Ninety-three police officers killed themselves in the 1930s when New York Mayor La Guardia attempted to clean up the notoriously corrupt police department. Many officers chose suicide rather than suffer the disgrace of an indictment. Today, there is still a high rate of suicide among police officers. In fact, more New York City officers die from their own hands than are killed by criminals. The reason is not usually corruption, but a combination of job stress and the available means—a loaded gun around their waist.

Ann Wickett Humphry

It bothered me that when I die I might slip through the cracks, and I thought, "Well, that's just the way it is." You live in the country and life is cheap. And maybe you finally have to accept the fact that you did slip through the cracks. I just want to get out of here and go to sleep and just be left alone. *From a videotape left by Ann Humphry*

With her husband Derek, Ann Humphry founded the Hemlock Society, a right-to-die group that publishes how-to books and campaigns for the liberalization of euthanasia laws. She was an active member, even helping her own parents commit suicide.

Then Ann was diagnosed with breast cancer. Four days after she began chemotherapy, Derek left a message on their answering machine saying their marriage was over. Depressed and dying, Ann began to contemplate suicide. It was an easy option because she had a healthy supply of barbiturates, courtesy of the Hemlock Society. But since committing suicide was so easy, she began to doubt the premise of the right to die movement.

Ann began to attack Derek and the Hemlock Society publicly. She continued the attack, long after her cancer went into remission and the threat of dying passed, using her final act as a prime argument against the movement.

But when she saw just how easy her suicide would be, she realized the danger inherent in the right-to-die movement. A perfectly healthy but emotionally disturbed individual like herself could commit suicide using the know how meant for the terminally ill.

But Ann's hate-filled note, excerpted below, makes one question her motives. Is she expressing serious doubts about euthanasia, or is she simply seeking revenge on her husband?

Derek:

There. You got what you wanted. Ever since I was diagnosed as having cancer, you have done everything conceivable to precipitate my death . . .

You will have to live with this until you die.

May you never, ever forget.

Ann

After her suicide, Derek Humphry responded with a half-page ad in *The New York Times.* "Sadly, for much of her life, Ann was dogged by emotional problems, and . . . her life was a series of peaks and troughs. Suicide for reasons of depression has never been part of the credo of the Hemlock Society. . . . *What organization does not have casualties? Emotional illness knows no boundaries.*"

3

To the Point?

No Comment
An anonymous note

Every imaginable way to leave a suicide note has been tried. They have been hand-written, typed, spoken and videotaped. They have been written in pen, pencil, crayon, blood, lipstick, chalk and dirt. They have been addressed to friends, lovers, family, the press, even pets. They have been mailed and e-mailed, left on answering machines or pinned to the body. They are two words or two thousand words.

These short notes particularly demonstrate the tremendous variety of final communication. Some say a lot in a few words; others offer only confusion.

To my friends:
My work is done.
Why wait? G. E.
From George Eastman, founder of Eastman Kodak

Bow wow and good-bye, Pepper
From a man to his dog

I'm done with life
I'm no good
I'm dead
From a fifty-year-old Massachusetts man

God forgive me.
A minister scrawled this note before hanging himself in his church. He wrote the note on the paper that the rope was packaged in.

Researchers have tried to correlate every imaginable variable with suicide. Here are some of the findings.

• Most suicides occur between the hours of noon and six P.M.
• There is an association between the moon and suicide. The peak isn't around the full moon, but around the new moon.
• Coffee drinkers are less likely to commit suicide.
• Suicide attempts for women are more common during menstruation and the days directly preceding it.
• Women who use birth control pills attempt suicide more often than those who use a diaphragm.
• Males with tattoos are more likely to use guns in their suicide, while those with brown eyes are more likely to choose hanging or poison.

I would like my sister Frances to have the piano that you have in your apartment. Do this or I will haunt you. Goodbye Sweets, Be seeing you soon. Love. Joe.
A man to his ex-girlfriend

Sorry about this. There's a corpse in here. Please inform police.
Before hanging himself, a workman chalked this on the wall of a home
he was repairing.

Kids, if there are any errors in this letter, I did not proof it carefully.
A teacher to the end, the superintendent of the Cleveland public schools
left this postscript to his note. His body was found in his school office
with a self-inflicted bullet wound.

Car to Helen or Ray. Needs a tuneup. Money to Max and Sylvia.
Furniture to George plus $137 I owe him.
A note from a thirty-year-old psychiatrist

Notes with mundane instructions are fairly typical. Researchers have
found that almost one-third of all notes contain practical requests—
everything from what to say on the tombstone to reminders to buy birthday gifts. These petty reminders signal that the writer is concentrating
on the smallest of details rather than on the larger implications of the
suicidal act.

Live fast, live well, die handsomely.
A man wrote this on a piece of cardboard before shooting himself.

Somebody had to do it. Self awareness is everything.
This note was found on a telephone message board next to the body of
a commodities broker. He had shot himself.

The job has got pressure on my mind, pain on my left side.
From a Midwest banker disturbed by having to foreclose on his friends. Before he turned the gun on himself, he shot his wife, two children, and his dog.

This is my Independence Day—from life. Love and Holidays are not for me. I'm tired and no one wants me.
A note left by a twenty-year-old woman on the Fourth of July

Merry Christmas
This note was pinned to a teenage boy who hanged himself behind a Christmas tree.

Many people falsely believe that the suicide rate increases around holidays. In fact, researchers have found that the lowest suicide rate of the year is in the festivities-filled month of December. Unfortunately many depressed people still find holidays too much to bear.

The most difficult time for the depressed is not the winter holidays but the spring months of May and June. In the first warm and sunny months after a cold and dark winter, the suicide rate is at its highest. This surprising finding may be because suicide does not usually occur at the worst phase of depression, but when the sufferer is beginning to get better. The spring thaw may be spiritual as well as literal, awakening the depressed into action.

4

Disgrace

Whether caught committing a crime, facing military defeat, or simply not living up to one's expectations, disgrace is a frequent reason for suicide.

Major Hubert Henry

French intelligence knew they had a spy. Major Hubert Henry was convinced it was a Jewish officer named Dreyfus who was betraying Catholic France. He had no evidence, so he fabricated incriminating evidence. The case exposed the deep roots of French anti-Semitism and sent Dreyfus to jail. When the story finally unraveled, the good officer Henry committed suicide. He left this note to his wife:

> *My adored Berthe, I see that except for you everyone is going to abandon me and yet you know in whose interest I acted. My letter is a copy and contains nothing, absolutely nothing, of a forgery. It merely confirms verbal information I had been given a few days earlier. I am absolutely innocent, they know it, and everyone will know later on; but right now, I can't speak. Take good care of our adored little Joseph, and continue loving him as I love you.*

Good-bye, my darling; I hope you will be able to come see me soon. I embrace you both from the very bottom of my heart. . . .

My beloved Berthe, I am like a madman; a frightening pain is gripping my brain. I am going to take a swim in the Seine. . . .

Charles Stuart

One hundred years after Dreyfus, little has changed. A husband and his pregnant wife are driving home from childbirth class. As they leave Boston's inner city on their way to the suburbs, they are car-jacked by an African-American man. He fatally shoots the pregnant wife and severely wounds the husband. Racial tensions mount as the white community's fears grow. Then the true story unravels. Charles Stuart's brother confesses that it was actually Charles himself who committed the crime. The next day, a disgraced Stuart jumps off Boston's Tobin Bridge. This note, with Stuart's driver's license placed on top, was found in his car.

To my family and friends,
I love you very much.
Thank you for standing beside me.
My life has been nothing but a battle for the last four months.
Whatever this new accusation is, it has beaten me.
I've been sapped of my strength.
Chuck

Both Henry's and Stuart's notes are remarkable for what they don't mention—an admission of guilt. There is no hint of remorse and no trace of confession. Instead, these suicide notes of disgrace are permeated by a feeling of persecution. Both Henry and Stuart are beleaguered victims, sapped of their strength and simply unable to continue fighting.

Other suicides of shame include:

- Judas. He did not leave a note.
- Jeff Alm, defensive tackle for the Houston Oilers. When Alm lost control of his Cadillac, his longtime friend was thrown through the window and killed. Seeing what he had done, Alm took out his shotgun and killed himself—without pausing to leave a note.
- Dan White, murderer of San Francisco's Mayor Moscone and gay supervisor Harvey Milk. White used the "Twinkie" defense at his trial, claiming that his addiction to junk food affected his judgment. The defense was successful in lessening the charge, but his suicide indicates he remained tormented by his crime.

Dr. Paul Kammerer

Biologist Paul Kammerer challenged Darwin's ideas with his own theory of evolution. Kammerer based his theory on a unique species of toad that could change the color of its paws. Then it was uncovered that Kammerer or someone in his lab was injecting ink into their paws. Filled with shame, Kammerer walked into the Austrian foothills and shot himself.

Letter to whosoever finds it:
Dr. Paul Kammerer begs not to be brought home, in order that his family be spared the sight. Simplest and cheapest would be to use the body in a university dissecting laboratory. I would actually prefer to render science at least this small service in this way. Perhaps my esteemed colleagues will find in my brain a trace of the qualities they found missing from the expressions of my intellectual activities while I was living.

Whatever happens to the corpse—buried, burned or dissected— its owner belonged to no religion and wishes to be spared a religious ceremony, which probably would be refused anyhow. This is not to show animosity against any individual priest who is human like everybody else and often a good and noble person indeed.

Kammerer penned a classic note of shame. His writing is filled with so much self-disgust, he no longer considers himself a human being. He is the owner of a corpse that no one will mourn, that doesn't deserve a burial, and that should be disposed of in the cheapest way. As with other notes of guilt, he admitted no wrongdoing.

Stephen Ward

Stephen Ward, doctor, painter, and lover of prostitutes, found himself in trouble when he "introduced" the same call girl to both a prominent British official and a Soviet official. The resulting scandal nearly toppled the British government, which subsequently prosecuted Ward for being a pimp. During the trial, he took an overdose of Nembutal, leaving this note to a friend.

Dear N.

I am sorry I had to do this here! It is really more than I can stand—the horror, day after day at the court and in the streets.

It is not only fear, it is a wish not to let them get me. I would rather get myself. I do hope I have not let people down too much. I tried to do my stuff but after Marshall's summing up, I've given up all hope. The car needs oil in the gear-box, by the way. Be happy in it. Incidentally, it was surprisingly easy and required no guts.

I am sorry to disappoint the vultures. I only hope this has done the job. Delay resuscitation as long as possible.

Ward's note became illegible as the drugs took effect. His request to delay resuscitation was ignored, and he died in the hospital four days later.

Adolf Hitler

> *My wife and I choose to die in order to escape the shame of over-throw or capitulation. It is our wish for our bodies to be cremated immediately on the place where I have performed the greater part of my daily work during twelve years of service to my people.*
> —From the suicide note of Adolf Hitler

Defeated political and military leaders often kill themselves rather than surrender. Their suicide helps them avoid the humiliation of capture, and as a final grasp at power to say "you didn't kill me, I killed myself."

Hermann Göring

Hermann Göring, founder of the Gestapo, the Nazi secret police, was captured at the end of the war, tried at Nuremberg, and sentenced to die by hanging. Refusing to give the Allies the satisfaction of execution, he took his own life with cyanide he had hidden in a 9 mm cartridge. Many believe that Göring kept the cartridge hidden in his anus during his months of captivity. Laboratory inspection did find fecal traces on the cartridge, suggesting he may have placed it there briefly, but given the cartridge's large size, he could not possibly have kept it there for long. Scholars suspect that a sympathizer supplied Göring with the vial at the last moment. Before poisoning himself, Göring left these three notes.

> *To the Allied Control Council:*
> *I would have let you shoot me without further ado! But it is not possible to hang the German Reichsmarschall! I cannot permit this, for Germany's sake. Besides, I have no moral obligation to submit to the justice of my enemies. I have therefore chosen the manner of death of the great Hannibal.*
> *It was clear from the outset that a death sentence would be*

pronounced against me, as I have always regarded the trial as a purely political act by the victors, but I wanted to see this trial through for my people's sake and I did at least expect that I should not be denied a soldier's death. Before God, my country, and my conscience I feel myself free of the blame that an enemy tribunal has attached to me.

Dear Pastor Gerecke!

Forgive me, but I had to do it like this for political reasons. I have prayed long to my God and feel that I am doing the right thing. (I would have let them shoot me.) Please comfort my wife and tell her that this was no ordinary suicide, and that she can rest assured that God will still gather me up in his great mercy!

God protect my dearest ones!

God bless you, dear pastor, evermore.

Your Hermann Göring.

My only sweetheart!

Upon mature consideration and after profound prayers to my God, I have decided to take my own life and thus not allow my enemies to execute me. I would always have accepted death by firing squad. But the Reichsmarschall of Greater Germany can not allow himself to be hanged. Moreover, the killings were to be carried out like a spectacle with the press and film cameras there (I assume for the newsreel pictures). Sensation is all that matters.

I however want to die quietly and out of the public eye. My life came to an end the moment I said my last farewell to you. Since then I am filled with a wondrous peace and I regard death as the final release.

I take it as a sign from God that throughout the months of my imprisonment He allowed me the means to free myself from this mortal coil, and that this means was never discovered. In His charity, God thus spared me the bitter end.

All my thoughts are with you, with Edda, and all my beloved friends! The last beats of my heart will mark our great and eternal love.

Your Hermann

Although written under the threat of execution, Göring's note bears remarkable resemblance to other suicide notes. He is fixated on a minor matter, the difference between hanging and the firing squad, and he uses the twisted logic of a suicide to justify his act. Since the Allies decided to hang him instead of shoot him, he rationalizes poisoning himself.

The similarity in the logic and language of all suicide notes may reflect the common frame of mind needed to kill oneself. Regardless of the individual reasons, all suicides must somehow convince themselves to commit an act that contradicts their innate desire for self-preservation.

O. J. Simpson

Accused of murdering his wife, the football great put a gun to his head and threatened suicide. Though he didn't pull the trigger, he did release this letter excerpted below, which bears remarkable resemblance to a suicide note of disgrace.

To Whom It May Concern:

First, everyone understand: I had nothing to do with Nicole's murder. I loved her, always have and always will. If we had a problem, it's because I loved her so much.

Unlike what has been written in the press, Nicole and I had a great relationship for most of our lives together. Like all long-term relationships, we had a few downs and ups.

I don't want to belabor knocking the press but I can't believe what is being said. Most of it is totally made up. I know you have a job to do, but as a last wish, please, please, please leave my children in peace. Their lives will be tough enough.

I want to send my love and thanks to all my friends—I'm sorry I can't name every one of you—especially A. C. Man, thanks for being in my life.

I think of my life and feel I've done most of the right things. So why do I end up like this? I can't go on. No matter what the outcome, people will look and point. I can't take that. I'm proud of how I lived. My momma taught me to do unto others. I treated people the way I wanted to be treated. I've always tried to be up and helpful. So why is this happening? I'm sorry for the Goldman family. I know how much it hurts. Nicole and I had a good life together. At times I have felt like a battered husband or boyfriend, but I loved her. Make that clear to everyone . . .

Don't feel sorry for me. I've had a great life, great friends, please think of the real O. J. and not this lost person. Thanks for making my life special. I hope I helped yours.

Peace and love, O. J.

Please, please, please, leave my children in peace.

O. J. Simpson's letter shares many similarities with suicide notes of disgrace.

- His very first line is the classic denial. He then paints himself as a victim, an innocent man persecuted by an overzealous press.
- Simpson uses the word *love*, which is ever so popular in suicide notes. Given his past record of domestic abuse, love must have a multitude of meanings for Simpson.
- Simpson's note provides many indications that he will soon be ending his life. He gives a long list of good-byes and uses such telling phrases as "a last wish" and "I can't go on." He even talks about himself in the past tense, as if he were already dead.
- "The real O. J." disassociates himself from "this lost person." This psychological split may give O. J. the emotional distance he needs to contemplate suicide.

> Suicide from shame is often because of wrongdoing. But many of the psychologically disturbed feel that they are a disgrace, even if they've never committed a crime. They too leave notes of shame—but theirs are permeated with self-hatred.

There's only one genius in a number of generations. My [father] is it. The next one can't be expected for 100 years. I've tried to live up to it. I can't. He ranks. I don't.

From a young man who shot himself. This note contains shame as well as anger toward his father. Another note was in his pocket that indicates he may not have understood the finality of the suicide. "Call N. M. tomorrow afternoon for dinner if conscious."

I have long determined that the best thing I could do was to put an end to the existence of a being whose birth was unfortunate and whose life has only been a series of pains to those persons who have hurt their health in endeavoring to promote her welfare.

Perhaps to hear of my death may give you pain, but you will soon have the blessing of forgetting that such a creature ever existed.

Fanny Imlay Godwin, the half-sister of Mary Shelley, the author of *Frankenstein,* wanted a number of things she did not have, including money and Mary's husband, the poet Percy Bysshe Shelley. This note is a classic of self-loathing shame.

As suicide expert Edwin Shneidman writes, "The key words in this painful note are 'being' and 'creature.' She is not a woman or a person or a human; she is just a biological thing that never should have been born. This is a note filled with nothingness; an overpowering sense of void and worthlessness."

I am food for what I am good for—worms. I have made a will here which I desire to be respected, and add the donation of £20 to Dr. Ecklin my physician. W. Beddoes must have a case (50 bottles) of Champagne Moet 1847 growth to drink my health in. . . . I ought to have been among other things a good poet. Life was too great a bore on one peg and that a bad one. Buy for Dr. Ecklin above mentioned Reade's best stomach pumps.

This excerpt is from the suicide note left by the poet Thomas Lovell Bedoes. Bedoes writes disparagingly about his poetry, even though many now consider his best-known work, the bizarre and grotesque *Death's Jest Book,* to be a classic.

Most people end their lives because something sad has happened to them. I end mine because it seems not only futile but wrong to go on existing. I blame no one and feel I have no enemies. I will probably be considered insane as anyone taking his life is supposed to be slightly insane.

I would like to send my regards to Miss S. in Drew Seminary. My check for $175 in the suitcase in the closet at home may help pay my burial expenses. I am very happy now.

I am wondering if the newspapers will decide to devote any space to me. I am wondering if I will find time to think of the past as I whirl through space as it is said that a drowning man does when struggling in the water. I am wondering if I will find anything in death. If so, what?

Everything has always been discord when I long so for harmony. Maybe yet, I will find it, maybe sweet music.

If I find any sort of life or corresponding time after death, I will try to communicate with my immediate relatives at nine o'clock some evening for a while. During my lifetime, I think my one fault was deception. I have lied repeatedly about small things, but unfortunately I forget what these small things were. I have no guilty conscience whatsoever.

From a note found in the purse of Ruth R. At 2,000 feet she opened the cabin door of a small plane, stepped out, and became the first person to commit suicide from an airplane.

- The writer's concern with the press is a reminder that suicide is often a public act. By choosing a dramatic exit, jumping out of a plane, Ruth probably hopes or expects someone will write about her. In a sense, the note is part of her publicity package.
- In her wonderment about the future, she presumes an existence past her death. Many suicides don't understand that death is permanent.
- Not all suicide notes offer an honest glimpse into a person's final moment. Here, the writer's intention may not be honesty, but clearing her name or erasing her guilt. Ruth says, "I have lied repeatedly about small things, but unfortunately I forget what these small things were." The true reason Ruth killed herself is unclear, but most likely there is a lie she remembers all too well. This is probably a suicide of disgrace.

5

Altruistic Suicide

Like cherry blossoms
In the spring
Let us fall
So pure and radiant.

From the final hiaku of a twenty-two-year-old kamikaze pilot. The kamikaze is the most famous example of altruistic suicide.

Scientists call taking one's life for a greater good *altruistic suicide*. Emile Durkheim coined the phrase and theorized that most suicides arise from an abnormal connection to society. The lonely, the failed, and the depressed kill themselves because they feel estranged from society. The altruistic suicide is the exact opposite; the individual has such an exaggerated sense of duty to his community, he will sacrifice his own life. Western society considers altruistic suicides mentally ill. It is hard to believe that people can hold convictions so strong they are willing to die for them. In other societies, though, these suicides are honorable; the line between what is admirable and what is insane seems to be culturally defined.

... My life is complete except all my brothers are in trouble—war, poverty, hunger, hostility.
My purpose is to make them understand all this trouble.
Maybe this will start a chain reaction of awakening, love, communication.
I've been so down, so god dam down, I can't get up. Not even pot helps ...

    Love and peace.

Craig B. and his girlfriend, two emotional teenagers protesting the Vietnam War, came to the conclusion that their dying message would be a more forceful protest than living speech. After a rally on October 17, 1969, they drove to a deserted area where they ran a vacuum cleaner hose from their tailpipe into their car. They left twenty-four letters on the dashboard calling for peace and an end to the war. This excerpt is from Craig to one of his closest friends.

In the 1960s, it was widely reported that protest suicides were a product of mental illness. Surely anyone who could kill himself as a protest must be unstable. But in this note, is there any sign of disturbance? One line does seem to show the depression and weariness common in many suicide notes: "I've been so down, so god dam down, I can't get up."

War and Peace

During the 1960s, some Vietnam War protesters chose to kill themselves to promote peace. In the 1990s, Arab suicide bombers attempted to kill the enemy Israelis in their holy war. Are these suicide notes for war and peace categorically different?

MY INTENTION
I wish to use my body as a torch
To dissipate the darkness

> *To waken Love among men*
> *And to bring Peace to Viet Nam.*

A teacher in Saigon burned herself in front of a pagoda with a picture of the Virgin Mary and the Buddhist goddess of mercy by her side. Fire is often the method of choice for protest suicide because it attracts attention and symbolizes purification.

> *I'm giving my life, not in war, but to help end it. If giving my life will*
> *shorten the war by even one day, it will not have been in vain.*

Ronald B. at age sixteen set fire to himself to protest the Vietnam War.

> *I have carried out my act of immolation as a protest against Johnson's*
> *war in Vietnam. The war is, like my final act, a war of frustration.*

John C., a four-year Navy veteran, set himself on fire in 1967.

> *I did it because I cannot adapt myself to this world. I did it as a sign*
> *of protest against violence, to see love again.*

The French teenager who wrote this note immolated himself to protest his country's involvement in Biafra. His reasons seem to go beyond protest.

> *The life of this world is just a game and an accumulation of posses-*
> *sions and children. What God has is better for me than all this.*

Hisham H. killed three Israeli soldiers on his suicide mission.

> *I am a future martyr. I do what I've decided to do with my soul at my*
> *peace. I do my duty for the love of my people and my country.*

Seventeen-year-old Sana M. blew up two Israeli soldiers with her bomb-laden Peugeot.

I saw many people around me from my country make mistakes, so I thought that the only way for me is to erase those mistakes through fighting the Israeli enemy.

Wafa Nour E. set off a suitcase full of explosives at an Israeli checkpoint.

Islam will be victorious in the end and lead the world. A true believer knows that if he demands death, he will be given a dignified life with all that it means.

Salah S.'s suicide mission killed nineteen and wounded sixty-eight Israelis.

Holy war is our path. My death will be martyrdom. I will knock on the gates of paradise with the skulls of the sons of Zion.

Ayman R. wounded thirteen soldiers on his mission of death.

While the Koran forbids suicide, a radical interpretation promises instant paradise to those who die for the cause. While the suicide bomber gets fame, his family gets money—a stipend of $800 a month—as well as a promise to rebuild their house if it is destroyed by the Israelis in retaliation.

Family Good Will

The greater good of an altruistic suicide can include helping or protecting one's family. As these notes show, the greater good is just as likely to be imagined as it is real.

*I'm tired of everyone saying how much talent I've got. Uncle B. got
everything to live for. And if they find out he can use it and Uncle B.
wants it, I'm going to be his donor. I figure I could do more good for
him than myself.*

An unemployed salesman drove to a local hospital and committed suicide near the main door. He left a request to donate his heart to his older
brother, B., who'd been on a transplant waiting list for three years. Ten
minutes passed before a nurse noticed the body slumped over the steer-
ing wheel of his car, and it was too late to transplant his heart. From the
note, the act of altruism seems to have more to do with his own lack of
self-worth than his generosity.

*You are my children and I love you more than myself. A. is also my
child. I cannot knowingly allow her to be sexually abused. I have no
choice. I hope you understand. Be kind to each other. I'm sorry I
have to leave you alone. Love forever. Mom.*

A mother left these words to her surviving children. She had accused her
ex-husband of sexually abusing their four-year-old daughter, A. But the
judge ruled that the vindictive mother had brainwashed her daughter into
making the charges. Rather than share custody with her ex-husband, as
the judge ordered, the mother took her daughter with her into the garage,
looped a rubber hose from the tailpipe into the car window, and started
the car. To the end, the mother believed she was protecting her daughter
by killing her.

*For every act there is a cause. In this instance the act is justified, at
least, I believe so. The following statement will establish if my con-
tention is right or not. I have been practicing law in this State for thirty
years. Have been and still am connected with fraternal and other organizations. I have always received the esteem of my fellow men.*

*For several years I have been mistaken for another party, the
reason for which is a similarity of names and by being in the same
profession. My full name is Ernest P., and my offices are at 519 Mar-
ket Street, a lawyer by profession, aged fifty-seven, height five feet*

seven inches. The other person is younger and six feet in height but because of his name has been continually mistaken for me. As a fact, even people with whom I am in close contact at the Hall of Justice and the City Hall have often mistaken me for him.

A few days ago he was charged with a statutory charge. Under the law I give him the right of presumption of innocence. However, that does not eradicate the fact that since that time I have realized from actions of many people that they seem to be under the impression that I am the one involved. A victim of circumstance, to say the least. Some people even, thoughtlessly joking, have remarked about the charge involving this man.

It seems nothing could well be done to establish the fact that I am not involved in that statutory charge. The only way is to give it publicity and I feel the act I am about to do will solve the problem. Personally, I care not. My life has been lived. My family is of the highest moral character and I feel that a stigma would attach unless I let the public at large know, through this deed, that I am a victim of circumstance by reason of mistaken identity.

I have been brooding over this matter, and the seriousness of the matter involving this other man makes it mandatory that I, Ernest P., should protect the reputation of my family in the only available and possible manner. Respectfully submitted.

Ernest P., a San Francisco attorney, left this note to the press before poisoning himself. At the time of his suicide, an attorney with a similar name was awaiting trial on a prostitution charge. In Ernest P.'s distorted world, it makes perfect sense to commit suicide to clear his name. This absurd logic is typical of suicidal thinking. It makes the suicide seem rational, which is why he can leave a calm and reasoned argument for his own death—even if it is fallacious.

A. Alvarez writes, "The logic of suicide is different . . . Once a man decides to take his own life he enters a shut-off, impregnable but wholly convincing world where every detail fits and each incident reinforces his decision. An argument with a stranger in a bar, an expected letter which doesn't arrive, the wrong voice on the telephone, the wrong knock on the door, even a change in the weather—all seem charged with special meaning. . . ."

The logic of the suicide creates a tunnel vision, what psychologists call "constriction." In this rigid thinking, all roads lead to only one choice—there are no alternatives, no other answers. Suicide notes often reveal this thinking by using phrases like "this is the only way" and "I must do this."

Tunnel vision may be a requisite for suicide, for it allows the mind to justify and commit an inherently unnatural act. While tunnel vision may permit a successful suicide, it cannot permit clear thinking or good communication. It's no wonder that suicide notes, written when the mind is at its most constricted, are not insightful personal reflections on the meaning of life. As Edwin Shneidman writes, "In order to commit suicide, one cannot write a meaningful note; conversely, if one could write a meaningful note, one would not have to commit suicide."

My dearest

I have taken my life in order to provide capital for you. The IRS and its liens which have been taken against our property illegally by a runaway agency of our government have dried up all sources of credit for us. So I have made the only decision I can. It's purely a business decision. I hope you can understand that. I love you completely . . .

You will find my body on the lot on the north side of the house.
Alex C. battled the IRS for nine years over a disputed deduction. The battle cost Alex a $300,000 IRS fine and thousands of dollars in legal fees, not to mention his life. He committed suicide so his wife, Kay, could receive the insurance money and continue the fight against the

IRS. She did continue the battle and, shortly after his death, a judge ruled that the IRS had erred and the family owed nothing.

According to his wife, Alex was depressed, but by no means mentally disturbed. Alex tried every option available, until the only option he saw available was suicide. In his mind, it was a completely rational "business decision."

> We have the means to afford the best doctors, hospitals and around-the-clock home care to the end of our days, but neither of us wants that kind of life. Also it would consume a substantial part of our money, which through our will and through the mission work of our church is destined to help many young people throughout the world who may one day be able to help many more. We have no immediate family or heirs. In a sense, this legacy represents the final purpose of our lives. Goodbye for now.

This note was left by an elderly couple who preferred that their ten-million-dollar fortune go to charity rather than to medical bills.

While many suicides use altruism as an excuse, this couple seem to have committed a truly generous act. For those opposed to suicide, though, it raises a troubling question: What, if anything, was immoral in their death?

6

The Artistic Temperament

Men have called me mad, but the question is not yet settled, whether madness is or is not the loftiest intelligence—whether much that is glorious—whether all that is profound—does not spring from disease of thought—from moods of mind exalted at the expense of the general intellect. —*Edgar Allen Poe*

What benefits does mental illness offer? Recent studies have indeed shown some traits of madness to be conducive to original art. For example, manic-depressives use rhyme, alliteration, and idiosyncratic words more than other people. It is possible that in the manic state, people think more quickly, fluidly, and originally. "When we think of creative writers," Kay Jamison, professor of psychiatry, says, "we think of boldness, sensitivity, restlessness, discontent; this the manic-depressive temperament."

The cruel irony is that the same disease that may lead artists to greatness also keeps them from enjoying the fruits of their success.

There are many things I should like to write you about, but I feel it is useless.

From the last letter of Vincent Van Gogh, written to his brother Theo. Van Gogh killed himself at age thirty-seven, probably as a result of manic-depression. In an earlier fit of madness, he cut off his ear.

Lucy, pardonnez-moi.

The French artist Pascin slit his wrists and dipped his brush into his own blood to write this note to his model. Then to assure success, he hung himself.

I'm deeply sorry for you. I spent Christmas Eve alone in this apartment hearing the laughter and joy of neighbors. But it's impossible to go through it again. On a day like this everyone seeks the company of beloved ones. Here I am with nowhere to spend New Year's in anyone's company. It's simply my fault. Forgive me for such a vulgar note.

A Brazilian cartoonist left this note to his mother on New Year's Eve. As if going to a party, he shaved and got dressed in his best white suit. He then spread a blanket and pillow on the floor, turned on the gas from his stove, and lay down to die.

"I think wanting to write is a fundamental sign of disease and discomfort. I don't think people who are comfortable want to write . . ."

Kay Jamison, professor of psychiatry at Johns Hopkins University

Dr. Kay Jamison is the foremost proponent on the link between creativity and madness. Some of the evidence collected by her and her colleagues include:

- Writers are ten to twenty times as likely to suffer from depression and manic-depression.
- 38 percent of a sample of creative artists in Britain had been treated for mood disorders. A subsample of poets had an even higher rate, 50 percent.
- A study of abstract expressionist artists showed half suffered from depression or manic-depression and had a suicide rate thirteen times higher than expected. A study of blues musicians showed similar results.

Virginia Woolf

Virginia Woolf, the author of the classics *To the Lighthouse* and *Mrs. Dalloway,* suffered from manic-depression. She had at least three serious breakdowns, and facing a fourth, she committed suicide. On March 28, 1941, she wrote this note to her husband, left it on the mantel, and headed toward a nearby river. Forcing a large stone into her pocket, she entered the river and drowned.

Dearest,

I feel certain I am going mad again. I feel we can't go through another of those terrible times. And I shan't recover this time. I begin to hear voices, and I can't concentrate. So I am doing what seems the best thing to do. You have been in every way all that anyone could be. I don't think two people could have been happier till this terrible disease came. I can't fight any longer. I know that I am spoiling your life, that without me you could work. And I know you will. You see I can't even write this properly. I can't read. What I want to say is I owe all the happiness of my life to you. You have been entirely patient with me and incredibly good. I want to say that—everybody knows it. If anybody could have saved me it would have been you. Everything has gone from me but the certainty of your goodness. I can't go on spoiling your life any longer.

I don't think two people could have been happier than we have been.

Woolf pioneered a style of writing called *stream of consciousness* in which she explored the complex workings of her characters' minds. She strove to focus her reader's attention on the moment-by-moment experience of living. Like her novels, her suicide note effectively achieved this goal.

Woolf's moment-by-moment experience included manic-depression, a disease characterized by frantic highs and bleak lows. During a severe bout, she could not eat, sleep, or write, and was often suicidal. At times, she would have delusions, once hearing the birds sing in Greek

outside her window. Whether manic-depression led to her art is unknown; that it led to her death is certain.

Kurt Cobain

"Now he's gone and joined that stupid club."
   —Cobain's mother referring to the deaths of young rock stars such
as Jimi Hendrix, Janis Joplin, and Jim Morrison. Like Cobain, all were
dead by the age of twenty-seven.

Kurt Cobain and his band Nirvana are credited with inventing the
grunge sound. Noisy and messy, grunge resonated with the disaffected
youth, tired and suspicious of the greed and commercialism of the eight-
ies.

Nirvana sold millions of albums, but the success was not enough to
save Cobain. Trapped in a downward spiral of drug addiction and depression, he overdosed at least twice. The police, it seemed, were making regular appearances at Cobain's house, breaking up fights with his
wife, Courtney Love, and confiscating handguns and semiautomatic ri-
fles.

On April 5, 1994, Cobain locked himself in the room above his
garage and wrote a note to his wife, friends, and fans. He then put a shotgun to his head and blew his brains out. The blast was so powerful, police had to use fingerprints to identify the body. Two days after his body
was found, Cobain's wife Courtney Love recorded this message to his
fans. She read his suicide note, excerpted below.

*This note should be pretty easy to understand. All the wording's from
the Punk Rock 101 . . . I haven't felt the excitement of listening to as*

well as creating music, along with reading and writing for too many years now . . . I've tried everything that's in my power to appreciate it, and I do. God, believe me, I do . . . I must be one of those narcissists who only appreciate things when they're alone. I'm too sensitive. I need to be slightly numb in order to regain the enthusiasm I had as a child . . . There's good in all of us and I simply love people too much. So much that it makes me feel too fucking sad . . . I have it good, very good, and I'm grateful. But, since the age of seven, I've become hateful toward all humans in general . . . I'm too much of an erratic, moody baby! I don't have the passion anymore, and so remember, it's better to burn out than to fade away.

Peace, love, empathy, Kurt Cobain

While Cobain's note is interesting in its own right, his wife's reading added another dimension, the reaction of a survivor.

- In Love's readings she reacts to Cobain's note with sarcasm and anger, calling him an asshole and mocking his note.
- She asks why he didn't simply quit music instead of killing himself. Of course, that's the tragedy of suicide: everybody else can see other solutions except the suicide.
- Love calls Cobain's note a letter to the editor. She is referring to his detached, unemotional style that is common in suicide notes.
- Love ends her reading by saying to the crowd: "Just tell him he's a fucker, OK? . . . and that you love him."

The Werther Effect

"A 20-year-old man accidentally shot himself to death at his apartment while imitating the suicide of Kurt Cobain . . .

As his friends watched early Monday, the man propped a 12-gauge shotgun on the floor and knelt with his mouth over the barrel, Sgt. Jim Hanson said.

'He wasn't intending to hurt himself,' Sergeant Hanson said. 'He put the gun up to his head and said, "Look, I'm just like Kurt Cobain," and the gun went off.' "

Associated Press, December 6, 1994

Experts worried that the death of Kurt Cobain would lead others to commit suicide. It was not an unreasonable concern. For centuries, well-publicized suicides have spurred others to act. The most famous example occurred in the eighteenth century after the publication of Goethe's *The Sorrows of Young Werther* in which the protagonist kills himself. Soon the police were finding copies of the book next to suicides. The copycat phenomenon is now called the Werther Effect.

Researchers have found interesting evidence to support the Werther Effect. After Marilyn Monroe's death, the suicide rate jumped 12 percent.

A study of thirty-three well-publicized suicides found the suicide rate increased after twenty-six of them. The more publicity the suicide received, the greater the increase in the rate.

In addition to the increase in the suicide rate, researchers have found an increase in automobile and airplane crash fatalities after well-publicized suicides. This is probably not a coincidence. Many people try to disguise their suicide as accidents. One researcher estimates that up to 25 percent of all single car crashes are deliberate.

"I wish, Charlotte, to be buried in the dress I wear at present: it has been rendered sacred by your touch . . . My spirit soars above my coffin. I do not wish my pockets to be searched. The knot of pink ribbon which you wore on your bosom the first time that I saw you, surrounded by the children— Oh, kiss them a thousand times for me, and tell them the fate of their unhappy friend! I think I see them playing around me. The dear children! How warmly have I been attached to you, Charlotte! Since the first hour I saw you, how im-

possible have I found it to leave you! This ribbon must be buried with me: it was a present from you on my birthday. How confused it all appears! Little did I then think that I should journey this road! But peace! I pray you, peace!

"They [the pistols] are loaded—the clock strikes twelve. I say amen. Charlotte, Charlotte! farewell, farewell!"

This is an excerpt from the fictional suicide note in Goethe's *The Sorrow of Young Werther.* Goethe's story, which included this note, inspired a wave of suicides. But compared to the emotional distance of a genuine note, this note seems obviously fictional. So why did it inspire so many to suicide? A. Alvarez believes it was a function of the Romantic period where life and art became inseparable. "At the high point of Romanticism," Alvarez wrote, "life itself was as though it were fictional, and suicide became a literary act."

Heinrich von Kleist

The German writer Kleist was obsessed with suicide. It was said of him that there was not a letdown that did not lead to thoughts of suicide, and not a friend to whom he did not suggest they commit suicide together. He eventually found that friend in Henriette Vogel, who was dying from cancer. The two took a trip to the German countryside, made a picnic, and shot themselves. They left this note to a friend, the first part by Kleist, the latter part by Henriette.

Heaven knows, my dear and excellent friend, what strange feelings, half sad, half joyful, move us in this hour, as our souls rise above the world like two joyous balloonists, to write to you once more, for actu-

ally we had decided not to send our friends and acquaintances cards of leave-taking. It must be because we have thought of you in a thousand happy moments, because we have imagined a thousand times how you with your generous nature would have laughed (exulted) if you had seen us together in the green room. Ah, the world is a strange place! —It seems somehow fitting that Jettchen [Henriette] and I, two gloomy, woebegone people, who have always deplored their own coldness, should have come to love each other with all our hearts, and the best proof of it, I feel, is that we are going to die together.

Farewell, our dear, dear friend, and be very happy—it is said to be possible on earth. We for our part wish to know nothing of the joys of this world, we know and dream only of heavenly meadows and suns, in the light of which we shall stroll about with long wings on our shoulders. Adieu! A kiss from me, who am writing this, to Muller; tell him to think of me now and then, and to remain a valiant warrior of God against the diabolical madness that holds the world enchained.—

    H. v. Kleist

But how this whole thing came to pass
I'll let you know another time,
Today I'm in too great a hurry.

               Henriette

Farewell, my dear friends; in joy and sorrow remember two strange people, who will soon embark on their great voyage of discovery.

    H. v. Kleist

Kleist's note is filled with Romantic expressions such as "two joyous balloonists," and "heavenly meadows . . . with wings on our shoulders." His dreams of a grand voyage is in remarkable contrast to most suicides who think little of where they're going, only about escaping their psychological pain.

Henriette's note is considerably less romantic. She will tell her friend how this came to pass another time, but of course there will be no other time. She says she is in too great a hurry, but why does she need to rush to death? Most likely she does not want to reflect on her suicide for fear that she might not go through with it.

"You hate to think so, but suicide seems to help sell books."
—Walker Percy

Walker Percy is responding to the tremendous success of John Kennedy Toole's novel, *The Confederacy of Dunces*. The story of how the obscure novel came to be published is now legend. After receiving rejection after rejection, Toole, an unknown and unpublished author, commits suicide. His mother destroys his suicide note but takes up the cause, relentlessly pursuing a publisher for the novel. She, too, suffers rejection, until she forces the book on the writer Walker Percy, who convinces a small university press to take a risk. The novel has now sold many thousands of copies and has even won the Pulitzer Prize.

In retrospect, some critics now credit much of the book's remarkable success to the suicide legend. Perhaps we, as a society, are attracted to artists that have killed themselves. We may unconsciously encourage this behavior by rewarding it with success.

The Holocaust

I'm going to put myself to sleep now for a bit longer than usual. Call the time Eternity.
From the note left by writer and Holocaust survivor Jerzy Kosinski

Sometimes this genius goes dark and sinks down into the bitter well of his heart.
Poet Paul Celan underlined this sentence in a biography before drowning in the Seine.

Writers who have survived the Holocaust only to commit suicide later include Kosinski, Celan, Primo Levi, and Tadeusz Borowski. That so many chroniclers of the Holocaust killed themselves may say something about the impossibility of their task: as artists they were trying to describe the indescribable; they were trying to make sense of the nonsensical.

Perhaps all artists, facing the impossibility of their task, risk suicide. We expect our artists to probe deeply or to use the cliché, "plumb their depths." We expect them to cope with our darkness, the Holocaust, Hiroshima, not to mention rape, murder, and child abuse. Their introspection may simply be an occupational risk, no different than the risk a construction worker faces on a high-rise building.

Ralph Barton

Ralph Barton was an acclaimed cartoonist for *The New Yorker* magazine in the 1920s. On May 20, 1931, Barton dressed in his silk pajamas and climbed into his bed. He opened *Gray's Anatomy* to an illustration of a heart; and while holding a cigarette in his left hand, shot himself in the right temple. His maid found the body with a cigarette in one hand, a .25 caliber pistol in the other. It must have made a striking but gory picture, which is exactly what Barton wanted. A flamboyant artist, Barton choreographed his own suicide as his last great work of art.

Perhaps this ability to compose one's death is a reason so many artists kill themselves. Suicide provides a way for artists to control their own stories, place a dignified and coherent ending, and even make a statement with their death that they could not make in life.

Barton's suicide note is an intriguing document for it is a mixture of both blatant lies and terrible honesty. While it makes for entertaining reading, it is ultimately the sad document of a gifted artist who used his death as his last great work of art.

Obit

Every one who knows me and hears of it will have a different hypothesis to offer to explain why I did it. Practically all of these hypotheses will be dramatic and completely wrong. Any sane doctor knows that the reasons for suicide are invariably psychopathological and the true suicide type manufactures his own difficulties. I have had, on the contrary, an exceptionally glamorous life, as life goes; and I have had more than my share of affection and appreciation.

The most charming, intelligent and important people I have known have liked me, and the list of my enemies is very flattering to me. I have always had excellent health; but since my early childhood I have suffered from a melancholia, which in the last five years has begun to show definite symptoms of manic-depressive insanity.

It has prevented my getting anything like the full value out of my talent, and the past three years has made work a torture to do at all. It has made it impossible for me to enjoy the simple pleasures of life. I have run from wife to wife, from house to house and from country to country in a ridiculous effort to escape from myself. In doing so, I am very much afraid that I have brought a great deal of unhappiness to those who have loved me.

In particular, my remorse is bitter over my failure to appreciate my beautiful lost angel, Carlotta, the only woman I ever loved and whom I respect and admire above all the rest of the human race. She is the one person who could have saved me had I been savable. She did her best. No one ever ever had a more devoted or more understanding wife. I do hope she will understand what my malady was and forgive me a little.

No one thing is responsible for this and no one person—except myself. If the gossips insist on something more definite and thrilling as a reason, let them choose my pending appointment with the dentist or the fact that I happen to be painfully short of cash at the moment.

No other single reason is more important or less temporary.

After all, one has to choose a moment, and the air is always full of reasons at any given moment. I did it because I am fed up with inventing devices for getting through twenty-four hours a day and with bridging over a few months periodically with some beautiful interest, such as a new gal who annoyed me to the point where I forgot my own troubles.

I present my remains, with my compliments, to any medical school that fancies them or soap can be made of them. In them I haven't the slightest interest except that I want them to cause as little bother as possible.

XXXXXXX
I kiss my dear children—and Carlotta.

Barton singles out his ex-wife Carlotta, an actress and beauty queen who had remarried the playwright Eugene O'Neill. From all accounts, Barton hadn't loved her in years. He mentions her here probably to embarrass her and increase the publicity value of his suicide. Paradoxically adding lies may allow him to be more honest in other parts of the note. For example, the line "I did it because I am fed up with inventing devices for getting through twenty-four hours a day" rings with honesty.

Sylvia Plath

Please call Dr. Horder.

The suicide note left by Sylvia Plath. Dr. Horder was her psychiatrist. Though only one sentence, this note is actually quite revealing. Why call a psychiatrist, for he can only help patients who are alive? Perhaps Plath didn't expect to die or couldn't comprehend that a successful suicide meant death.

Dying
Is an art, like everything else.
I do it exceptionally well.

I do it so it feels like hell.
I do it so it feels real.
I guess you could say I've a call.

From Sylvia Plath's poem *Lady Lazarus.* Plath wrote constantly about death and suicide.

Sylvia Plath is synonymous with the term *suicidal artist.* She was a child prodigy, writing her first poem at age eight. But at age nineteen, the overachiever crashed hard with a nervous breakdown and a suicide attempt. As she chronicled in her autobiographical novel, *The Bell Jar,* she left a note that she was going for a walk and instead went to a hiding place in her basement. There, she swallowed fifty sleeping pills. It was practically a miracle that she was found still alive.

Plath regained her strength through poetry. But her poetry found its strength in her own private horrors of suicide, death, and depression. Thus Plath was caught in a catch-22. She need her poetry for her sanity, but she needed her insanity for her poetry. On February 11, 1963, she began what many say was an inevitable act. She started by protecting her children. She opened the window in their room and sealed the door with tape and towels. With her kids safe, she sealed herself in the kitchen, prepared a resting place near the oven, and turned on the gas. She wrote this poem about her impending suicide only a few days before she died.

Edge

The Woman is perfected.
Her Dead

Body wears the smile of accomplishment,
The illusion of a Greek necessity

Flows in the scrolls of her toga.
Her bare

Feet seem to be saying:
We have come so far, it is over.

Each dead child coiled, a white serpent,
One at each little

Pitcher of milk, now empty
She has folded

Them back into her body as petals
Of a rose close when the garden

Stiffens and odours bleed
From the sweet, deep throats of the night flowers.

Writing in *The Savage God,* Alvarez asks, Why did Plath kill herself? He answers: "In part, I suppose, it was a 'cry for help' which fatally misfired. But it was also a last desperate attempt to exorcise the death she had summoned up in her poems. . . . The more she wrote about death, the stronger and more fertile her imaginative world became. And this gave her everything to live for. I suspect that in the end she wanted to have done with the theme once and for all. But the only way she could find was 'to act out the awful little allegory once over.' She had always been a bit of a gambler, used to taking risks . . . Finally Sylvia took that risk. She gambled for the last time, having worked out that the odds were in her favour, but perhaps in her depression, not much caring whether she won or lost. Her calculations went wrong and she lost."

Anne Sexton

"We talked of death, and this was life to us."
   —Anne Sexton describing her friendship with Sylvia Plath. The two poets spent many hours discussing the details of their suicide attempts.

Anne Sexton, like her friend Sylvia Plath, fought a losing battle with mental illness. Hers began after the birth of her second daughter, a condition doctors call post-partum depression. Distraught and suicidal, she had to be committed to a hospital. One day her therapist suggested she write about her problems. Soon, the mad housewife was a poetry star.

She said her poems "read like a fever chart for a bad case of melancholy." They were fashioned out of her chaotic life, her mental breakdown, her anguish and her preoccupation with death. They struck a nerve with both critics and everyday people. And they garnered every major award including the Pulitzer Poetry Prize.

Sexton's world began to crumble when her long-time therapist moved out of town. Though she started treatment with a new doctor, their relationship turned sexual, destroying her marriage in the process. With her two main supports gone, she drifted aimlessly. She became addicted to alcohol and sleeping pills and drove away her remaining friends and family. On October 4, 1974, at the age of 45, she was found dead in her garage with her car still idling.

Though she left no formal note, her poetry constantly probed suicide and death. This poem, "Wanting to Die," is from her Pulitzer Prize–winning collection *Live or Die*.

Wanting to Die

Since you ask, most days I cannot remember.
I walk in my clothing, unmarked by that voyage.
Then the almost unnameable lust returns.

Even then I have nothing against life.
I know well the grass blades you mention,
the furniture you have placed under the sun.

But suicides have a special language.
Like carpenters they want to know which tools.
They never ask why build.

Twice I have so simply declared myself,
have possessed the enemy, eaten the enemy,
have taken his craft, his magic.

In this way, heavy and thoughtful,
warmer than oil and water,
I have rested, drooling at the mouth-hole.

I did not think of my body at needle point.
Even the cornea and the leftover urine were gone.
Suicides have already betrayed the body.

Still-born, they don't always die,
but dazzled, they can't forget a dung so sweet
that even children would look on and smile.

To thrust all that life under your tongue!—
that, all by itself, becomes a passion.
Death's a sad bone; bruised, you'd say,

and yet she waits for me, year after year,
to so delicately undo an old wound,
to empty my breath from its bad prison.

Balanced there, suicides sometimes meet,
raging at the fruit, a pumped-up moon,
leaving the bread they mistook for a kiss,

leaving the page of the book carelessly open,
something unsaid, the phone off the hook
and the love, whatever it was, an infection.

With her line, "But suicides have a special language/ Like carpenters they want to know which tools/ They never ask *why build*," Sexton describes a universal truth of suicides. So focused on how to commit the act, they fail to step back and ask the more important question, why.

John Berryman

I am a nuisance.

The note John Berryman wrote to his wife before attempting suicide.

John Berryman won practically every poetry prize there was to win, including the Pulitzer Prize and the National Book Award. Despite his success, Berryman was deeply insecure. He thought he was a terrible lecturer and a poor poet who faced imminent dismissal from the university. Insecurity is one of the inherent dangers of being an artist. Even successful artists face constant criticism, rejection, and financial uncertainty. Though he had been trying to kill himself for years with alcohol, he set out on January 5, 1972, to make a formal attempt. His plan was to slit his throat and jump off a bridge into the Mississippi, but he could not bring himself to die. He wrote the poem "I Didn't" about his attempt, but threw it in the trash before he finished. Two days later, on January 7, 1972, "he did and he did," jumping off the bridge, though not slashing his throat. A witness said he waved good-bye.

I didn't. And I didn't. Sharp the Spanish blade
to gash my throat after I'd climbed across

the high railing of the bridge
to tilt out, with the knife in my right hand
to slash me knocked or fainting till I'd fall
unable to keep my skull down but fearless

unless my wife wouldn't let me out of the house,
unless the cops noticed me crossing the campus
up to the bridge
& clappt me in for observation, costing my job—
well, I missed that;

but here's the terror of tomorrow's lectures
bad in themselves, the students dropping out of the course,
the Administration hearing
& offering me either a medical leave of absence
or resignation—Kitticat, they can't fire me—

Dorothy Parker

Dorothy Parker was known as the wittiest woman in New York. Though her poems and short stories are indeed humorous and clever, they also have a dark side, with thoughts of depression and death. She titled her first book of poetry *Enough Rope,* and she wrote lines like "If I had a shiny gun, I could have a world of fun." She attempted suicide as many as five times. Before taking an overdose of barbiturates, she left this "last will and testament."

Any royalties on my books are to go to John McClain, my clothes and my wrist watch to my sister, Helen Droste, also my little dog, Robinson.

Parker's list of instructions offers a glimpse of what she considered important in her life—her royalties, her clothes, her watch, and her dog. Of course, with Dorothy Parker, these may reflect her wry humor more than her true feelings.

Parker survived this suicide attempt, as well as all her others. Her message remains as a rare note of a survivor. Most destroy the evidence of an incident they'd rather not remember.

Suicide experts consider attempters to have less suicidal intent than completers, but is there any indication of this in Parker's note? Parker's message fits the common pattern of a suicide note as a simple set of instructions. As in many of these notes, her requests may seem innocuous but are an attempt to control the survivors. For example, Parker leaves her royalties to her erratic lover, John McClain, most likely in an attempt to instill a lasting guilt.

Parker's note does seem genuine. In fact, formal studies comparing attempted and completed suicide notes have shown few differences.

As Dorothy Parker grew older, she turned to alcohol, practically stopped writing, and reportedly talked more to her poodle than to her friends. She also stopped trying to kill herself. She died at the age of seventy-three of a heart attack. Perhaps she had taken the advice of her famous poem on suicide.

Résumé

> Razors pain you;
> Rivers are damp;
> Acids stain you;
> and drugs cause cramp.
> Guns aren't lawful;
> Nooses give;
> Gas smells awful;
> You might as well live.

Sergei Esenin

Farewell, my friend, without handshakes or words,
Don't be sad and don't frown in sorrow—
In this life, to die is not new,
But to live, of course, is less so.

Written in his own blood, this is an excerpt from the last poem of the great Russian poet Sergei Esenin. Esenin had been a lifelong alcoholic who suffered from delirium tremens and hallucinations. Drunk, disturbed, and lonely, he wrapped a rope around his neck, kicked the night table from under his feet, and hanged himself.

Ken Kesey

Ken Kesey gained instant fame with the publication of *One Flew Over the Cuckoo's Nest*. The novel, with its tales of mental illness and suicide, came from his personal experience working at a psychiatric hospital. While he was no stranger to lunacy, Kesey also had an infatuation with drugs. He had discovered the hospital's supply of hallucinogenics and wrote most of *Cuckoo's Nest* while tripping. He later invested his book profits into promoting the wonders of LSD, going so far as to organize huge psychedelic parties called Electric Kool-Aid Acid Tests. The police eventually cracked down on Kesey, arresting him for drug possession (as well as assaulting a police officer and resisting arrest). Facing certain jail time, Kesey skipped bail. Four days later, on February 6, 1966, his bus was found parked near the ocean with this note inside.

Last Words
   A vote for Barry [Goldwater] is a vote for fun.
   Ah, the Fort Bragg sign and that means the ocean and that means time to drop the acid (not that I really need it, mind you; I've

courage enough without chemical assistance, it's just that I'm scared . . .)

> *Driving along, check the abyss at my left like I'm shopping for real estate prospects. Ocean, ocean, ocean. I'll beat you in the end. I'll go through with my heels at your hungry ribs.*

> *I've lost the ocean again. Beautiful, I drive hundreds of miles looking for my particular cliff, get tripped behind acid. I can't find the ocean, end up slamming into a redwood just like I could have slammed into a home. Beautiful.*

> *So I Ken Kesey being of (ahem) sound mind and body do hereby leave the whole scene to Faye, corporation, cash, the works. And Babbs to run it. (And it occurs to me here that nobody is going to buy this prank and now it occurs to me that I like that even better.)*

No one did believe Kesey's note, for obvious reasons. A warrant was issued for his arrest and Kesey fled to Mexico. Seven months later, he returned to California for one last Acid Test. He was spotted and caught after a brief chase down the San Francisco Freeway. Though he was sentenced to seven months in jail, the suicide ploy and his capture only added to Kesey's legend.

7

In Public

Forcing others to watch death sends a strong and gruesome message. But the following notes from some public suicides show that the message is usually far from obvious. Is it publicity, revenge, or the sheer joy of exhibition?

Bud Dwyer

This has been like a nightmare, like life in the twilight zone. It wouldn't surprise me to wake up this minute to find out I was home in my bed and had just had a terrible nightmare. That's how unbelievable this has been. I mean, I've never done anything wrong . . .
From Bud Dwyer's farewell speech, January 22, 1987

Caught red-handed accepting a bribe and facing fifty-five years in jail, Bud Dwyer, the Pennsylvania state treasurer, called a news conference. Reporters expected Dwyer to announce his resignation; instead, he delivered a long, rambling speech proclaiming his innocence.

When he finally finished the speech, he handed his aides three envelopes. One contained instructions for his funeral, another held his organ donor card, and the third was a letter to the governor with the absurd request to appoint Dwyer's wife as the new state treasurer.

Then Dwyer pulled a .357 Magnum revolver from a manila envelope in his briefcase. Several reporters ducked for cover. There were shouts of "Bud, don't do this," and "Oh God." Dwyer kept the reporters at bay, waving the gun and saying, "Please leave the room as this will . . . as this will hurt someone." He then put the barrel of the gun into his mouth and fired.

This is the final page of Dwyer's twenty-one-page speech.

I've repeatedly said that I'm not going to resign as state treasurer. After many hours of thought and meditation, I've made a decision that should not be an example to anyone else, because it is unique to my situation.

Last May I told you that after the trial, I would give you the story of the decade. To those of you who are shallow the events of this morning will be that story. But to those of you with depth and concern, the real story will be what I hope and pray results from this morning—in the coming months and years, the development of a true justice system here in the United States.

I am going to die in office in an effort to "see if the shameful facts, spread out in all their shame, will not burn through our civic shamelessness and set fire to American pride." Please tell my story on every radio and television station and in every newspaper and magazine in the U.S. Please leave immediately if you have a weak stomach or mind, since I don't want to cause physical or mental distress.

J, R, D—I love you! Thank you for making my life so happy. Goodbye to all of you on the count of three. Please make sure that the sacrifice of my life is not in vain.

- Dwyer had prided himself as an honest politician, yet was caught accepting a bribe. The contradiction between his ideals and his actions was too great and he literally imploded.
- As is typical of suicides of disgrace, Dwyer portrayed himself as a martyr and refused to admit his guilt. But if he was guilty, and the evidence was incontrovertible, why make it a public suicide? The answer is revenge.
- But if he was guilty, in Dwyer's mind, the press had hounded him,

treated him unfairly, and in the end brought about his demise. Making them witness his violent and bloody death was just payback. As psychiatrist John Fryer said at the time, "To do it this way is to really get back at everybody and make sure nobody will escape."

Christine C.

"Wouldn't it be neat if I were to take the gun, pull it out on the air, live and blow myself away."
Christine joking to a friend a week before her suicide.

Christine was the host of a light morning talk show called *Suncoast Digest*. On the morning of July 15, 1974, her station introduced a new, hard news format. As Christine read a report on a shoot-out at a bar, mechanical trouble developed with the film clip. The camera returned to Christine. She smiled and said:

In keeping with Channel 40's policy of bringing you the latest in blood and guts in living color, we bring you another first, an attempted suicide.

She reached into a shopping bag behind her desk, pulled out a .38 revolver, pointed it at the lower back of her head, and pulled the trigger. Her body slumped forward and the screen went black.

Christine's suicide can easily be ascribed to mental illness, for she had been depressed and suicidal. Buried beneath the madness, though, was a powerful indictment of television. She was giving the station just the kind of news they wanted.

The Golden Gate Bridge

More than a thousand people have taken the plunge from America's number-one departure site. Obvious reasons for the bridge's popularity are that it is easy and effective, but there must be something more, for many suicides travel over the equally effective and accessible Oakland Bridge just to jump off the Golden Gate.

Perhaps jumping from a popular site is a way of committing a public act. Many suicides are lonely and estranged from society, so sharing an experience with thousands links them in death to a community they never had in life. It may even make it seem like one is not dying alone.

This is where I get off.
The last words of Harold W., the first person to jump off the Golden Gate Bridge. W. leapt in August 1937, a mere three months after the bridge opened.

Absolutely no reason except I have a toothache.
The note from forty-nine-year-old John Thomas D.

The survival of the fittest. Adios Unfit.
The note from a seventy-two-year-old man

$36
The amount of money found in the mouth of a jumper. What he meant by this gesture is open to interpretation.

I am sorry . . . I want to keep dad company.
The note left by twenty-four-year-old Charles G., Jr., whose father had jumped from the bridge four days earlier

Do not notify my mother. She has a heart condition.
From Steven H., the 500th person to jump off the bridge. There was no need to tell his mother, for she saw it on the evening news. The 500th suicide had been greatly anticipated. Fourteen people vied to have the dubious honor, with one even stenciling the number 500 on his T-shirt.

Why do they leave this so easy for suicide? Barbed wires would save a lot of lives.

From a note left by a seventy-year-old man

"For people depressed and impulsive, the Golden Gate Bridge is like having a loaded gun around the house."

—Psychologist Richard Seiden

Indeed, the only thing separating the public from plunging to death is a four-foot railing. While there are constant calls to install barriers, they have been rejected due to cost and aesthetics. It's a shame, since former suicide magnets, such as the Empire State Building and the Eiffel Tower, have installed barriers and practically eliminated suicides.

Instead, the bridge is closely watched. Police regularly patrol the area and employees watch through TV monitors looking for potential jumpers—men in suits are the most obvious. They've also installed telephones directly to suicide counselors, though they are rarely used.

Many jumpers do want to be dissuaded from suicide. In fact, one readily surrendered after a police officer pulled his gun and said, "Get down or I'll shoot." Unfortunately, in another case, an officer shot a suicidal man at the railing after he looked like he was drawing a gun.

Those who aren't deterred fall 223 feet, about 12 stories, and hit the water at 80 mph. Only about twenty people have survived. Most drown or die of internal injuries.

I and my daughter have committed suicide.

The simple note left by a man who jumped with his five-year-old daughter

For the past six or seven years I have been enduring the slings and arrows of outrageous misfortune until I feel like a worn-out pin

cushion. My mood is one of profound discouragement and my personal future appears bleak.
The note left by a fifty-seven-year-old attorney

I have simply come to the point of despair. My mind refuses to think clearly, and I am not able to cope. I wish with all my heart and soul there was some other way out of this terrible torment. My last and loving thoughts are of you.
From a note from a California lawyer to his wife

Loved Ones: My nerves are shot. Please forgive me. Chris
A note from Chris C., a member of the San Francisco board of supervisors. He turned up alive a year later selling Bibles in Houston. It was the first of many fake suicides from the bridge.

A study of bridge jumpers found the following:

• Jumping increases on full moons and holidays.
• Jumping is a local phenomenon. Only 5 percent come from outside the San Francisco Bay Area.
• Jumpers are getting younger. Once the average was over fifty; now it's less than thirty.
• The most famous jumper: Roy Raymond, founder of Victoria's Secret clothing chain.
• The most misguided: the man who jumped because he didn't get into Columbia Law School—only Stanford.

Vince Foster

A depressed Vince Foster may not have wanted to commit suicide in the public eye, but his role as deputy White House counsel and his friendship with President Bill Clinton made his pain a public matter.

Foster's note was found torn into twenty-seven pieces at the bottom of his briefcase. It is common for suicides to destroy their notes, since many who feel they are unworthy to live also feel their final thoughts aren't worth sharing.

I made mistakes from ignorance, inexperience and overwork

I did not knowingly violate any law or standard of conduct

No one in the White House, to my knowledge, violated any law or standard of conduct, including any action in the travel office. There was no intent to benefit any individual or specific group.

The FBI lied in their report to the AG [attorney general]

The Press is covering up the illegal benefits they received from the travel staff

The GOP has lied and misrepresented its knowledge and role and covered up a prior investigation

The Ushers Office plotted to have excessive costs incurred, taking advantage of Kaki [White House Designer] and HRC [Hilary Rodham Clinton]

The public will never believe the innocence of the Clintons and their loyal staff.

The WSJ [Wall Street Journal] editors lie without consequence

I was not meant for the job or the spotlight of public life in Washington. Here ruining people is considered sport.

Suicide notes are often one-sided arguments that cry out for a response. Because Foster was a public figure, his note demanded a public accounting. Foster may have even felt his suicide was the only way to air some of these issues. Indeed, Foster's suicide note may be the first to have ever received a point-by-point response in the press.

The *Wall Street Journal,* which Foster singled out, faced considerable scrutiny. They had published several highly critical editorials on Foster and the White House counsel. Its last attack was published six days before his suicide.

In a direct response to the note, a *Wall Street Journal* editor said, "There is no way to cover national government on the assumption that a high official and steeled litigator secretly suffers from depression and may commit suicide if criticized. What we said about Mr. Foster was nothing compared to the abuse heaped on the likes of Ed Meese, Robert Bork, and Clarence Thomas."

Vince Foster suffered from the number-one cause of suicide, depression. Over 70 percent of all self-inflicted deaths can be traced to this debilitating disease. Far from the everyday blues, clinical depression is overwhelming and inescapable. Involuntarily, the victims become so focused on their pain that they can think of little else. They will try anything for relief, including suicide.

Some believe that Foster was murdered to cover up White House wrongdoings. This cry of murder arises with every famous suicide, from Marilyn Monroe to Kurt Cobain. People who aren't depressed simply find it hard to believe that those who have so much to live for would ever want to kill themselves.

Vince Foster, at the top of his career, showed clear signs of depression. In the weeks before his suicide, he lost his appetite, developed insomnia, had trouble concentrating, and spoke of feeling worthless. His depression was so bad that he was placed on antidepressant medication.

The pettiness of his note is also an indication. The references to petty political disputes indicate that, in the midst of a severe emotional crisis, Foster could not put his problems into perspective. Many sufferers of depression face this problem and leave as evidence notes full of trivia and inconsequential details. "One of the hallmarks of depression," says writer and depression sufferer William Styron, "is the way it causes its victims to magnify troubles out of proportion to their true nature. Paranoia reigns, harmless murmurings are frightened with menace, shadows become monsters."

Through his own experience with depression, Styron realized that politics had little to do with Foster's suicide. "It was not Washington that became the real proscenium for Vincent Foster's tragedy," he wrote. "It was the stage inside the mind upon which men and women enact life's loneliest agony." And the note is simply a tortured artifact of the diseased mind.

Virtual Suicide

The Internet offers a new venue for public suicide. On a particularly morbid bulletin board individuals post their suicide notes, ask for technical advice on how to do the job right and lament on the general weariness of life. Far from a lonely death, people can now kill themselves with the entire wired world watching.

Many suicide notes cry out for response, but can't be answered until it's too late. But virtual notes can be responded to—and that seems to be the point. These writers have taken the suicide note as communication to a logical extension, full dialogue. Many in fact seem more interested in the conversation than the act.

Critics call this bulletin board pornography, suicide turned into interactive entertainment. That may be a knee-jerk reaction to the frightening nature of some of the postings, not to mention the poor taste. But virtual suicide may actually be a healthy phenomenon. Suicide offers many benefits—communication, revenge, catharsis and sympathy. Of course it has one really big drawback. With virtual suicide you get everything without the dying.

The following is a collection of postings. It is impossible to know how many of these postings are "legitimate" or how many writers go on to attempt suicide.

Subject: It's time to die . . .
> *I'll be killing myself soon. Consider this my Suicide Note. I may kill myself within the next few days. If not, I'll post a few more times . . . (I posted this at Xmas time, But I think most of you that frequent this place were "gone home" for the holidays. (as only a couple responded).*

This writer decided to post his suicide note again because he didn't get a suitable response the first time.

Subject: a really long note. Please proofread and post corrections.
> *Well here is my not so little contribution to the group. I would hope that someone could help me proofread it. Remember, "A 'friend' is the sort of person you could safely entrust the proofreading of your suicide note to. There are depressingly few of them out there." I figure that if I'm going to be remembered for one act it might as well be done to perfection. Anyway here goes:*

The writer received advice on her writing style including an admonishment to avoid contractions.

Subject: Internet Suicide Note
> *. . . What's sad is that it didn't have to end like this. I had so much potential ten years ago. So many people thought I would go straight to the top. But now I'm so isolated that will never happen. I don't want the Cheryl Crow nude pic. All I want is a hug dammit! But I'll never have another one . . .*

Subject: Re: Internet Suicide Note
> *{{{{{{{{{{{{{{{}}}}}}}}}}*
> *(hug for you)*

Some psychologists worry that suicidal people may not be getting the professional care they need via the computer. The response to this note may not meet accepted psychiatric practice. But there does seem to exist a genuine camaraderie on the internet. Questions are answered and problems are taken seriously. The virtual world may offer a community that many depressed people lack in the concrete world.

8

Hollywood Endings

I am afraid I am a coward.
I am sorry for everything.
If I had done this a long time ago, it would have saved a lot of pain.

The note left by Peg Entwistle, a failed actress, who jumped from the top of the famous Hollywood sign. She chose the letter H and fell five stories to her death.

Hollywood is a tough place for the psyche. Constant rejection, an abnormal focus on youth and appearance, and a steady supply of drugs do not make for ideal mental health. That some stars, seeing their beauty, talent, or celebrity disappear, choose suicide is no surprise.

TO ALL I LOVE,
Do not grieve for me—my nerves are all shot and for the last year I have been in agony day and night—except when I sleep with sleeping pills . . . I have had a wonderful life but it is over and my nerves get worse and I am afraid they will have to take me away . . . The future is just old age and pain . . . My last wish is to be cremated so nobody will grieve over my grave—no one is to blame.
Jimmy

James Whale, director of *Frankenstein* and *The Invisible Man*. The only time he used his swimming pool was to drown himself.

> *Dear World:*
> *I am leaving because I am bored. I am leaving you with your worries in this sweet cesspool.*

Actor George Sanders, who won an Oscar for the movie *All Above Eve*. He had four wives and seven psychiatrists.

Marilyn Monroe was the most famous Hollywood suicide. On August 4, 1962, she took an overdose of barbiturates. She had attempted suicide twice before and had been deeply depressed. She left no suicide note.

Other Hollywood suicides include Superman (George Reeves), *Wizard of Oz*'s Auntie 'Em (Clara Blandick), and *Fantasy Island*'s Tattoo (Herve Villechaize). The dwarf actor Villechaize left a note that he was frustrated with his tiny body.

Many celebrities commit what researchers call chronic suicide. They don't consciously kill themselves, but instead engage in continuous self-destructive behavior, such as drug use, drinking, and reckless driving. The deaths of actors James Dean, John Belushi, River Phoenix, and many rock stars fit this mold.

Freddie Prinze

Freddie Prinze, the nineteen-year-old star of *Chico and the Man,* turned to drugs to help him cope with his overnight success. He took as many as seven Quaaludes a day and snorted so much cocaine that he burned a hole in his nostril. Desperate to get high, he inserted cocaine in his rectum. Then Prinze bought a gun for protection, and it soon became his favorite plaything. He would spend hours loading and unloading it, putting it in his mouth, and staging mock suicides. Prinze was emotionally unstable, and the breakup of his marriage pushed him over the edge. On January 28, 1977, he made some final calls and penned this note.

I must end it.
There's no hope left.
I'll be at peace.
No one had anything to do with this.
My decision totally.

Freddie Prinze.

A concerned friend, D, responded to Prinze's phone call and arrived at the door. Prinze asked if his suicide note was legible and then added one more line to it.

P.S. I'm sorry. Forgive me. D's here. He's innocent. He cared.

Prinze grabbed for his gun. D tried to dissuade him, but Prinze pulled the trigger.

Prinze's note is remarkably unrevealing, but it seems to have held deep meaning to him. Not only did he take the time to write it, he asked his friend if it was legible. Many suicides take great pains to leave a note, without realizing how little their note actually communicates.

Lupe Velez

Actress Lupe Velez was known in Hollywood as the "Mexican Spitfire." Perhaps her nickname came from her sharp temper or from her ability to burn through men. But after a devastating divorce from *Tarzan*'s Johnny Weismuller, Velez never recovered. Her career, her self-esteem, and her bank account took a downward spiral. Then she found out she was pregnant by her latest lover, Harald Ramond. With Ramond unwilling to marry and Velez unwilling to get an abortion, she decided on the most extreme solution.

Lupe Velez decided to craft one last dramatic scene. She ordered a fabulous Mexican feast; then, like a Hollywood set designer, she decorated her bedroom with satin sheets, flowers, candles, and a large crucifix. With seventy-five Seconals and a suicide note, the scene was complete.

> *To Harald,*
>
> *May God forgive you and forgive me, too but I prefer to take my life away and our baby's before I bring him with shame or killin him.*
>
> *LUPE*

On the other side:

> *How could you, Harald, fake such a great love for me and our baby when all the time you didn't want us? I see no other way out for me so goodbye and good luck to you.*
>
> *Love,*
> *LUPE*

Velez is clearly indicting Ramond for her death and her note is meant to induce lasting guilt. Her phrase "good bye and good luck to you" are no doubt sarcastic. In a sense, this is what Ramond said to her when he chose not to marry her. And it is what Hollywood said to Velez, who at thirty-six was at the end of her beauty and her career.

The day after her suicide, the Hollywood gossip columnists reported the beauty of Velez's final scene, but in reality, her movie had a very different ending. The Seconals didn't mix well with the Mexican food. Police found a trail of vomit leading to the bathroom. Inside, Velez was facedown in the toilet. She had slipped on the tiles, fallen into the toilet, and drowned.

Paul Bern

> *Dearest Dear,*
> *Unfortunately this is the only way to make good the frightful wrong*
> *I have done you and to wipe out my abject humiliation. I love you,*
> *Paul*
> *You understand that last night was only a comedy.*

From the suicide note of Hollywood screenwriter and producer Paul Bern. The note was addressed to his wife, the beautiful actress Jean Harlow. When the sex goddess Harlow was unable to cure Bern of his impotency, he shot himself. According to Hollywood insiders, Bern's "abject humiliation" refers to his impotency and the fact that his sex organ was the size of a child's. Last night's "comedy" was rumored to be his attempt to penetrate Harlow with a dildo.

While there was some intrigue surrounding Bern's death, the autopsy was consistent with a self-inflicted gunshot wound. His sex organ was also examined: the conclusion—"developed normally, but undersized."

9

Suicide Diaries

The reasons to keep a diary are many: some write for understanding, others have an eye toward posterity. When the writer kills himself, the diary becomes a long-term, day-by-day suicide note.

Cesare Pavese

A man who ejaculates prematurely should never have been born . . .
it is a defect that makes suicide worthwhile.

Cesare Pavese, one of Italy's most acclaimed postwar writers, kept a diary from 1935 to 1950. Excerpts from his last year of life show his pathway to suicide.

Suffering from premature ejaculation and possibly impotence, Pavese had trouble satisfying women. His strange coping mechanism was to reject the women who loved him and pursue the women who rejected him. This is the case with the young American actress Constance D., with whom Pavese became obsessed. Referring to her frequently in the last year of his diary, he seemed to be deliberately setting himself up for failure. He staked his happiness on her, knowing he would never win her over; therefore he could never be happy.

In the strange entry of May 27, Pavese wonders whether he should kill himself out of friendship or revenge—for a woman who he barely knows! Even at the most rewarding moment of his career, when he wins Italy's most prestigious writing award, the Strega Prize, he must write of her absence. But in a rare moment of insight on August 16, he does admit to himself that she is only a pretext for a deeper problem—the "agonizing disquietude" of depression.

January 14, 1950
I am filled with distaste for what I have done, for all my works. A sense of failing health, of physical decadence. The downward curve of the arc . . .

March 23
Love is truly the great manifesto; the urge to be, to count for some-thing, and, if death must come, to die valiantly, with acclamation—in short, to remain a memory. Yet my desire to die, to disappear, is still bound up with her: perhaps because she is so magnificently alive that, if my being could blend with hers, my life would have more meaning than before.

March 25
One does not kill oneself for love of a woman. One kills oneself be-cause love—any love—reveals us in our nakedness, our misery, our vulnerability, our nothingness.

May 8
The cadence of suffering has begun. Every evening at dusk, my heart constricts until night has come.

May 16
Now even the morning is filled with pain.

May 27
My happiness of '48–'49 is paid for in full. Behind that Olympian contentment lay my impotence and my refusal to become involved.

Now, in my own way, I have gone down into the abyss: I contemplate my impotence, I feel it in my bones, and I am caught in a political responsibility that is crushing me. There is only one answer: suicide.

Dilemma. Should I act in perfect amity, doing it all for her own good, or diabolically explode? A pointless question—already settled by my whole past, by fate: I shall be a diabolical friend, gaining nothing by it—but perhaps I shall have the courage. The courage. Everything will depend on having it at the right moment—when it will do her no harm—but she must know it, she must know it. Can I deny myself that?

Certainly, I know more about her than she does about me.

May 30
All these lamentations are far from stoical. So what?

June 22
[after learning that he will win the Strega Prize, Italy's top writing award]
. . . This journey looks like being my greatest triumph. Social acclaim, D. will talk to me—all the sweet without the bitter. But then? What then?

Do you know that the two months have passed? And that, at any moment, she may return?

August 16
. . . Today I see clearly that from '28 until now I have always lived under this shadow . . . even you are only a pretext. The real fault, apart from my own, lies with that "agonizing disquietude, with its secret smile."

I have done my part by the world, as best I could. I have worked; I have given poetry to men, I have shared the sorrows of many.

August 17
Suicides are timid murderers. Masochism instead of sadism. . . . This is the balance sheet of an unfinished year, that I won't finish.

August 18.

[Pavese's last entry]

The thing most feared in secret always happens.

I write: oh Thou, have mercy. And then?

All it takes is a little courage.

The more the pain grows clear and definite, the more the instinct for life asserts itself and the thought of suicide recedes.

It seemed easy when I thought of it. Weak women have done it. It takes humility not pride.

All this is sickening.

Not words. An act. I won't write anymore.

Pavese uses his last entry as a way to prepare himself for the act. He also realizes that if he continues to write, he may talk himself out of suicide. To kill himself, Pavese must stop writing.

A week later, Pavese goes to an Italian newspaper office and picks out his obituary photograph from the photo archive. He then checks into a hotel and calls three or four women friends. No one will join him. On August 27, a worried hotel employee finds Pavese stretched out on the bed, fully dressed except for his shoes. On his nightstand are sixteen empty packets of sleeping pills and a copy of his book, *Dialogues with Leuco,* opened to the first page with this note:

I forgive everyone and ask forgiveness of everyone. O.K.? Not too much gossip, please.

B. R. Haydon

Benjamin Haydon was a nineteenth-century painter of Britain's historic past. Today he is more famous for his diary than for his art. Haydon's diary is filled with his financial problems. He has trials for debt and is often fighting off bill collectors. But in his entry of June 16, despite the weight of his problems, one can feel his love of painting and his joy at finding the perfect model.

Haydon's journal filled twenty-six volumes, so he obviously had no want of things to write about. But his last days are strangely silent. He doesn't write on the nineteenth and just a few lines on the twentieth, twenty-first, and twenty-second. Whatever is stirring in his head, he is unable or unwilling to communicate. Haydon is clearly in turmoil over the impending act. In his rambling and incoherent last thoughts, he has come to the conclusion that he is evil for not having paid his bills.

June 15th.— Passed in great anxiety; finally painted the background in the sketch, after harassing about to no purpose in the heat.

16th.— I sat from two till five staring at my picture like an idiot. My brain pressed down by anxiety and anxious looks of my dear Mary and children, whom I was compelled to inform. I dined, after having raised money on all our silver, to keep us from want in case of accidents; and Rochfort, the respectable old man in Brewer Street, having expressed great sympathy for my misfortunes, as I saw white locks under his cap, I said, "Rochfort, take off your cap." He took it off, and showed a fine head of silvery hair. "This is the very thing I want: come and sit." He smiled, and looked through me. "When?" "Saturday at nine." "I will, sir"; and would any man believe, I went home with a lighter heart at having found a model for the hair of the kneeling figure in Alfred? This is as good as anything I remember of Wilkie in my early days. I came home, and sat as I describe.

18th.— O God, bless me through the evils of this day. Great anxiety. My landlord, Newton, called. I said "I see a quarter's rent in thy face; but none from me." I appointed to-morrow night to see him, and lay before him every iota of my position. "Good-hearted Newton!" I said, "don't put in an execution!" "Nothing of the sort," he replied, half hurt.

I sent the Duke, Wordsworth, dear Fred's and Mary's heads to Miss Barrett to protect. I have the Duke's boots and hat, and Lord Grey's coat, and some more heads.

20th.— O God, bless us all through the evils of this day. Amen.

21st.— Slept horribly. Prayed in sorrow, and got up in agitation.

22nd.—God forgive me. Amen.

Finis

of

B. R. Haydon.

"Stretch me no longer on this rough world."—Lear

End of Twenty-sixth Volume

Haydon's body was discovered in his studio by his daughter. His throat had two slashes and his head had one bullet. He left on a table his diary with its last entry, an open prayer book, and this note.

Last thoughts of B. R. Haydon, half-past ten:

No man should use certain evil for probable good, however great the object. Evil is the prerogative of the Deity.

I create good, I create, I the Lord do these things.

Wellington never used evil if the good was not certain. Napoleon had no such scruples, and I fear the glitter of his genius rather dazzled me; but had I been encouraged nothing but good would have come from me, because when encouraged I paid everybody. God forgive the evil for the sake of the good. Amen.

Haydon left his diary near his body where it would obviously be found.

One may think that a diary contains one's most intimate thoughts. But many journals like Haydon's seem to have been written with the public in mind. Far from private, the diary seems designed for others.

Lee Harvey Oswald

I am shocked! * * * I have waited for 2 year to be accepted. My fondes dreams are shattered because of a petty offial, * * * I decide to end it. Soak rist in cold water to numb the pain, Than slash

my leftwrist. Than plaug wrist into bathtum of hot water. * * * *Some-
where, a violin plays, as I watch my life whirl away. I think to myself "How easy to Die" and "A Sweet Death, (to violins)* * * *

This entry comes from the diary of President John F. Kennedy's assas-
sin.

Fearing deportation after Oswald defected to the Soviet Union in
1959, he attempted suicide. His diary, which he self-importantly titled
"Historic Diary," has a painfully public tone to it. Thomas Mallon, a his-
torian of diaries, calls Oswald's language "tacky rhetorical finery. . . .
Oswald seems to have read just enough books to remember and occa-
sionally approximate the 'literary' tone appropriate to dramatic happen-
ings to the hero."

Kenneth Halliwell

If you read his diary all will be explained.
K. H.
P.S. Especially the latter part

This suicide note was left by Kenneth Halliwell, who before taking his
own life, bludgeoned his lover, the playwright Joe Orton, with a ham-
mer. The diary Halliwell is referring to is Orton's—in which he describes his play writing triumphs, his anonymous public bathroom sex,
and his troubles with Halliwell.

Leaving someone else's diary as a suicide note is a strange twist. It's
as if Halliwell, so full of self-loathing, can't even write his own expla-
nation. As Thomas Mallon writes, "Thoroughly eclipsed by his lover
and victim, Halliwell even let him do the posthumous talking to the police. Instead of destroying Orton's humiliating version of their rotting
partnership, he called attention to it."

Diane Arbus

The Last Supper
The last entry scrawled into Diane Arbus's journal. Arbus, best known for her startling and bizarre photographs of dwarfs, transvestites, and freaks, slit her wrists in 1971.

There is a rumor that Arbus set up a camera to capture her suicide. No evidence of this photographic diary has ever been found.

Suicide Diaries: The Last Moments of Life

These remarkable journals come from the last moments of life. As the gas fills the room, the poison enters the bloodstream, these victims pen their progress to oblivion. Perhaps in this last desperate act of communication, they think the truth and understanding that eluded them during life will at last come.

More likely they write just to distract themselves from thinking about their terrible and difficult deed. The writers here remain detached and clinical, even when describing their deaths. In fact, it may actually be psychologically impossible to seriously reflect on the true meaning of the act and still go through with it.

Terrific smell of gas fumes . . . it would be 6:34 P.M. civilian time. It's getting rather dark to write. Eyes smart a bit . . . Afraid somebody will come by now . . . This is slow (6:36 P.M.)

Engine sounds smooth. Faculties seem temporarily sharpened. Eyes still smart . . . one man objected when I stopped on his property . . . can't blame him much really . . .

Seems that there are more gas fumes in here than anything else right now . . . muscles used in writing . . . in need of a rest. I'm afraid somebody will come.

Elbows, esp., and wrists. Where is the will? . . . No particular desire to get out . . . seems to be getting the better of me fast. It's been just 15 minutes now. I wonder what it's going to be like? Chest filling up fast. Seems to be terrific pressure first.

[Illegible scrawling]

From the diary of a twenty-one-year-old Massachusetts man, these notes were made as his car filled up with exhaust fumes.

Waiting. Feeling very happy. First time I ever felt without worry, as if I were free. My heart must be strong. It won't give way. . . . Extraordinary. Pulse running well. Feel fine—when will it be over? . . . God seems to be over me—just leaving for a lovely voyage, but it is slow—first time without worry.

This entry is from the journal of a British physician. Heavily in debt, he decided to poison himself. While he waited to die, he took the time to treat a number of patients.

I feel the effects now. The room is going around and around. I can barely see what I am writing. Maybe it is the end. Who knows? I don't care . . .

Written by a man as he is overcome by the bite of a black widow spider. The man went to great lengths to obtain the venomous spider.

Psychologists have long looked for meaning in the choice of suicide method, as George Howe Colt has compiled in his book *The Enigma of Suicide:*

• Freud thought the method of suicide was related to sexual wish fulfillment. For example, he thought women who poisoned themselves wanted to become pregnant.

- Analyst Wilhelm Stekel had his own theories: "Women who 'have fallen' or who struggle against temptations, throw themselves out of the window and into the street. The man who entertains secret thoughts of poisoning somebody, takes poison; one who yearns after the flames of love, sets fire to himself." Stekel must have secretly wished to poison someone, for he later committed suicide with an overdose of aspirin.
- Freudian Karl Menninger thought suicide by drowning was an attempt to return to the womb.
- Psychiatrist Joost Meerloo thought jumping out a window was somehow an attempt to grow up.
- Psychiatrists Sidney Furst and Mortimer Ostow hypothesize that homosexual males shoot themselves out of their desire to be attacked by a penis. They jump from tall buildings to express sexual guilt for "phallic erection under improper circumstances."

Suicides do send messages with their manner of dying. A man depressed by impotence blew himself up with a stick of dynamite and an opera teacher jumped from the balcony of the Metropolitan Opera House.

This is my last experiment and it is in self-destruction. I believe that it is advisable, if one's inclinations lead to the anti-social side.

I think Spinoza told the world more than Christ did, although Christ's message was more fundamental.

Enticing as personal immortality sounds, I hope for oblivion. The worst they can do for one in this world is to hang you, and if there is any eternal torment worse than mine I'll have to be shown.

I don't know if it is of much importance, but I feel that the only method of dying without pain is to use carbon monoxide. To get a supply I am passing city gas through concentrated sulphuric acid to delete the mercaptan odor.

There is no one that admires Jesus Christ more than I do, al-

though the conventional contemporary method of worshiping him gives me a pain in the neck.

P.S.: The question of suicide and selfishness to close friends and relatives is one that I can't answer or even give an opinion on. It is obvious, however, that I have pondered it and decided I would hurt them less dead than alive.

P.P.S.: and the eight balls dreadful, like an outhouse in a fog, looms up to charm its victim, supine in the grip of grog.

This chemist, suffering incredible torment, found his science skills useful for only one thing: to die a clean and efficient death.

10

Mass Suicide

Throughout history, groups have chosen collective suicide rather than surrender to their enemies. In ancient times, almost a thousand Jewish zealots barricaded at Masada chose to kill themselves rather than surrender to the Romans. In 1944, the entire Japanese city of Saipan committed suicide rather than submit to Allied troops. Soldiers blew themselves up with grenades while civilians walked off cliffs into the Pacific. Most recently, mass suicide seems to be the preferred exit for besieged religious cults, such as the Branch Davidians and the People's Temple.

Jim Jones and the People's Temple

Jim Jones was the charismatic leader of a religious cult called the People's Temple. Moving his followers from the United States to the jungles of Guyana, Jones promised a Communist utopia. Instead, he delivered a nightmarish hell.

A visit by Congressman Leo Ryan precipitated the tragic events. Ryan had been sent by irate parents to investigate the cult. He planned to take home a scathing report as well as twenty unhappy members. Before he could leave, Jones's followers ambushed the congressman, killing him and four of his entourage. Rather than face reprisals from the United States and the probable end of the People's Temple, Jim Jones prepared a batch of cyanide Kool-Aid.

It is a difficult scene to imagine: parents spooning poisonous punch to their babies, and then drinking it themselves; cries and screams; bodies collapsing; armed guards preventing any chance of escape; and all the while, Jim Jones exhorting his nine hundred followers to drink the poison. A tape recorder captured this final speech.

The audiotape contains a strange and eerie combination of sounds, from chilling cries and gagging children to outbursts of applause and cheers. The fact that it was recorded is in itself significant. The Guyana compound was tightly controlled, with guards surrounding all exits. The recording probably could only have occurred with the permission of Jones. Most likely he had this scene recorded on purpose as his message to the world, his evidence of martyrdom.

Jones: *I've tried my best to give you a good life. In spite of all that I've tried, a handful of our people, with their lies, have made our life impossible. There's no way to detach ourself from what's happened today . . . If we can't live in peace then let's die in peace.* [applause] *We've been so betrayed. We have been so terribly betrayed . . .*

So my opinion is that you be kind to children, and be kind to seniors, and take the potion like they used to take in Ancient Greece, and step over quietly; because we are not committing suicide—it's a revolutionary act. We can't go back; they won't leave us alone. They're now going back to tell more lies, which means more Congressmen. And there's no way, no way we can survive . . .

Well, some, everybody dies. Some place that hope runs out; because everybody dies. I haven't seen anybody yet didn't die. And I like to choose my own kind of death for a change. I'm tired of being tormented to hell, that's what I'm tired of. Tired of it. [applause] *. . .*

This is—what I'm talking about now is the dispensation of judgment. This is a revolutionary—a revolutionary suicide council. I'm not talking about self—self-destruction. I'm talking about that we have no other road. . . .

Please get us some medication. Simple. It's simple, there's no convulsions with it. It's just simple. Just, please get it. Before it's too late . . . I tell you, get movin', get movin', get movin'. Don't be afraid to die. You'll see people land out here. They'll torture our people. They'll torture our seniors. We cannot have this . . .

Woman: *. . . O.K. There's nothing to worry about. Everybody keep calm; and try and keep your children calm. And all those children that can help, let the little children in and reassure them. They're not crying from pain; it's just a little bitter tasting, they're not crying out of any pain . . .*

Man: *The choice is not ours now. It's out of our hand . . . It feels good, but never felt so good—I tell you. You've never felt so good as how that feels . . .*

Woman: *Good to be alive today. I just like to thank Dad* [Jim Jones] *'Cause he was the only one to stand up for me when I need him. I'm glad to be here . . .*

Woman: *I'm glad that you're my brothers and sisters. I'm glad to be here . . .*

Jones: *Mother, mother, mother, mother, mother please. Mother please. Please, Please. Don't do this. Don't do this. Lay down your life with your child. But don't do this. Free at last. Keep—keep your emotions down. Children, it will not hurt. If you'd be—if you'd be quiet. If you be quiet* [music and crying] *. . . So be patient. Be patient. Death is—I tell you, I don't care how many screams you hear; I don't care how many anguished cries, death is a million times preferable to spend more days in this life . . . Let's be digni—let's be dignified. If you quit telling them they're dying—if you would also stop some of this nonsense—adults, adults, I call on you to stop this nonsense. I call on you to quit exciting your children, when all they're doing is going to a quiet rest. I call on you to stop this now,* *if you have any respect at all . . . All they do is taking a drink. They take it to go to sleep. That's what death is, sleep—I'm tired of it all . . . Have trust. You have to step across. We used to think this world was—this world was not our home, and it sure isn't . . . Take our life from us. We laid it down, we got tired. We didn't commit suicide, we committed an act of revolutionary suicide protesting the conditions of an inhumane world.* [organ music]

Until the end of the tape, Jones remained remarkably calm, but it's clear that finally, the screaming and crying began to get to him. As the tape ran out, Jones shot himself.

Two days later, in a scene that overwhelmed the senses, the Guyanese forces found nine hundred men, women, and children rotting in the hot, humid jungle.

Many individual suicide notes seem to be designed to convince the mind of the necessity of the act. Using similar logic, Jim Jones structured his speech to convince almost a thousand people to follow him in death.

Here are some of the similarities between Jones's speech and a suicide note.

- Jones uses the distorted logic often present in suicide notes. He plans to protect his children by killing them.
- Suicide is seen as the only option. Like most suicides, he is so narrowly focused that he can see no other alternative. His language reinforces this with phrases like "we have no other road" and "It's the will."
- With lines like "We've been so betrayed" and "they won't leave us alone," Jones is blaming others for his problems. As in many suicides of disgrace, Jones takes no responsibility for the murders that have brought this crisis. Instead, he tries to portray himself and his followers as martyrs.
- Underlying the entire message is a sense of weariness with life. Jones uses phrases like "I'm tired of it all" and "living is difficult." No mat-

ter what the specific causes of a suicide are, this tired feeling shows up time and time again.

> *Dad—I see no way out—I agree with your decision—I fear only that without you the world may not make it to communism.*
>
> *For my part—I am more tired of this wretched, merciless planet & the hell it holds for so many masses of beautiful people—thank you for the only life I've known.*

This letter was found on one of the bodies. It is addressed to Dad, the name cult members used for Jones. It contains two of the more common elements found in suicide notes: a weariness of life and a belief that there is no other alternative.

> *I thought I should at least make some attempt to let the world know what Jim Jones and the People's Temple is—or was—all about.*
>
> *It seems that some people—and perhaps the majority of people—would like to destroy the best thing that ever happened to the 1,200 or so of us who have followed Jim. I am at this point right now so embittered against the world that I don't know why I am writing this . . .*
>
> *Much to the contrary of the lies stated about Jim Jones being a power hungry, sadistic mean person who thought he was God (of all things!) I want you who reads this to know JIM was the most honest, loving, caring, concerned person whom I ever met and knew . . .*
>
> *What a beautiful place this was . . . We die because you would not let us live in peace.*

This is from the note written by Jim Jones's personal nurse. There was speculation that she and perhaps other reluctant members were murdered. This note disproved that theory.

11

Around the World

The readiness of the Japanese to disembowel themselves for the slightest reason is well known.

—Emile Durkheim

Japan

Durkheim's stereotype of Japan is actually incorrect. While we may imagine that every overworked manager, failing student, and shamed politician will be the next statistic, the suicide rate is no different in Japan than in the United States and even less than in many European countries. Suicide seems more prevalent in Japan because of the dramatic methods such as hara-kiri and the kamikaze, that some use to kill themselves. In Japan it is also culturally acceptable to kill one-self for dishonor or for the greater good of the country. But if suicide is seen to be more rational and more accepted, are their notes any less unstable?

I feel disgusted when I see guys who make a fuss about the entrance examination all the time. Rebelling, I have not studied for about two months. I don't think I can pass. I am in bad shape. Therefore, I die, although I would like to enter a first-rate university. I am ashamed of myself, unable to grow out of childishness. I envy others. There should be room for a stupid man like me, too. I would like to see Hell. This note was left by an eighteen-year-old boy. It is estimated that 40 percent of youth suicide in Japan is due at least partly to the stress of college entrance exams.

Please stay calm. Try to hide my suicide. Please don't think about causes of my suicide and don't inquire about what I have done before death. For me the present university is nothing. If we go to a university in Japan, it must be Tokyo or Kyoto. Many people attend uninteresting classes for four years and wait for employment. It is just like cows and pigs waiting in a wooden stable to be pulled out to the slaughterhouse. I cannot stand it.

I believe in the fairy tale that I may be able to be reborn as a superior human being. Then I will enter Tokyo or Kyoto University, or even Sorbonne or Harvard.

A note left by a twenty-four-year-old male student

Not fulfilling your dream or hope, I am determined to kill myself. I cannot help dying with contempt for myself as the scum of society and an ungrateful coward. My mother's incessant but miserable efforts . . . all were beyond what I deserved. I don't know how to apologize to my mother. When I think of my hardworking mother, laboring without rest, I cannot die despite myself. I even think I should take her with me. For about two years, this kind of thought haunted my mind.

This note from a twenty-two-year-old student expresses his sense of guilt at failure, compounded by his family's poverty. In Japan, the poor are three times as likely to commit suicide.

. . . I have no will of my own. From now on, I cannot escape from the agony. Since I began feeling other people's minds, I have come to

feel even more miserable. I may look human from the outside, but my inside is empty, stupid, dull-witted and self-isolating. What on earth is in me? I may be breathing, thanks to the support of parents and other people around me, but my real self is like a lifeless doll.

This note is from a depressed Japanese woman whose fiancé had recently broken off their engagement when he found out his wife-to-be was burakumin, a lower caste group.

This is a demonstration of resistance to present-day Japan by a person who has wriggled for twenty-five years at the bottom of this society, because of his Korean ancestry.

This excerpt from a typical protest suicide note was left by a member of the Korean minority. Koreans are routinely discriminated against in Japan. They are ineligible to vote, have difficulty gaining entrance into schools, and suffer routine job discrimination.

Japanese suicide notes also seem remarkably similar to Western notes. The actual specifics may vary—a different type of failure, a different type of discrimination, a different type of societal pressure—but the feelings of self-loathing, disgrace, love, and hate that permeate these notes are the same.

Although its overall suicide rate is not extraordinary, Japan has one of the highest rates for women in the world. The reasons include a court system that makes divorce difficult, few job opportunities for women, and a culture that expects a woman to take the blame for the sins of her husband and children.

One area where Japanese attitudes seems to differ substantially from the West is the acceptance of altruistic suicide. The most famous example of Japanese sacrificing themselves for the good of the group is the kamikaze. It is also not unusual for a subordinate to sacrifice himself for the good of his company. During a scandal, a scapegoat will take

responsibility for wrongdoing, commit suicide, and thus end any criminal investigation. In turn, the company repays the favor by protecting and
rewarding the suicide's family. In the West, where company loyalty is
rare, these suicides seem ludicrous—and a changing Japan is beginning
to agree.

Taku Y.

Taku Y. helped his company smuggle millions of dollars of jewelry and
paintings into Japan and then use that money to bribe politicians for fa-
vorable contracts. When police investigations began, Taku Y. hanged
himself. He wrote this note to a member of the Japanese parliament.

*I thank you for the favor you have given me just because I am from
the same prefecture as you. I have regarded you as a god.*

*Since the revelation of this incident, you have given me kind sup-
port. I am thankful for it and I feel sorry that I gave you much trouble. You told me to be patient and endure . . . Please laugh at me
who could not be courageous enough to endure.*

*I saw many wrongdoings by the president and the director, and
I thought "just this much will be all right." Then I found myself the
whipping boy, as reported in newspapers and on television. I feel
something is wrong. I have been framed; I am the victim.*

*I cannot forgive the president and the director. They led me to
destroy the proof of their misdeeds, and still they behave as if they
have nothing to do with me. I cannot but feel angry.*

*You have told me not to have rancor against others, but the fact
is that the director bought jewelry, art, antiques, and paintings from
the department store. Why am I alone to be picked out? I have
worked hard in the matter of gift giving to outsiders. I took upon myself much trouble just for my company. And now I am the one who is*

blamed for everything. After all, I was stupid to be used, because I worked hard to adjust myself to the atmosphere in the president's room under the direction of the director. Please laugh at me.

May I take the liberty of asking your favor for my family members?

As Mamoru Iga argues in his book *The Thorn in the Chrysanthemum,* this note differs strikingly from what was once the typical sacrificial suicide note. Taku refuses to go quietly. He doesn't accept responsibility but instead incriminates his superiors. Far from helping his company, he uses his suicide to hurt it.

That attitudes are changing is also indicated by Japanese suicide rates. Cities now have lower rates than the more traditional rural areas, and even between cities, those known to have more Western attitudes have lower rates. As Japan becomes Westernized, sacrificial suicides may one day lose their acceptance.

Ryuunosuke Akutagawa

As with their western counterparts, Japanese writers have a propensity for suicide. Many have made suicide a central theme, and at least six of Japan's greatest writers have killed themselves, including Mishima, Arishima, Akutagawa, Makino, Dazai, and Kawabata.

Akutagawa is best known for his work *Yabu no Naka (In the Thicket),* which became the famous movie *Rashomon.* In this story, a woman is raped while her husband is forced to watch. The characters then retell the scene, but each offers a strikingly different view. The story is widely recounted as the most famous example of the illusion of truth. It typifies the skepticism and cynicism of Akutagawa's work.

Sadly Akutagawa suffered from mental illness. He began to have illusions: there were maggots in his food and people and dogs were laughing at him. In 1927, at the age of thirty-five, he took an overdose of sleeping pills. He left a note, excerpted below.

*. . . We humans are animals, and all animals are afraid of death.
What we call life energy is animal energy. But my being tired of eat-
ing and having sex must mean I am losing animal energy. The world
I am living in now is the icily transparent universe of sickly nerves.
I spent last night with a prostitute, talking about her wage. The talk
made me realize the misery of human beings, struggling just to live.
If we can enter eternal sleep, we may at least have peace, even if we
may not enjoy happiness.*

*However, I am doubtful about when I can dare to take my own
life. Under conditions like these, Nature herself looks more beautiful to me than ever. You may laugh at the contradiction between
the love of Nature and the wish for suicide. However, Nature looks
even more beautiful exactly because I am at the end of my life. This
gives me satisfaction even in a life which has been a series of suf-
ferings. Please do not publish this letter for several years after my
death. I may end my life in such a way that it appears to be death
from illness . . .*

*Of course, I do not want to die, but it is suffering to live. People
may laugh at me for committing suicide when I have parents, a wife
and children. If I were alone, I would not have committed suicide.
My wish to commit suicide now is probably the only willful act in my
life. I have had many dreams, as all young people do, but thinking
back, I might, after all, just have been an odd person. At present I
dislike everything, including myself.*

Akutagawa writes about the love of nature and the wish for suicide. This
connection has a long history. The Japanese choose dramatic settings so
often that is said, "Almost any place that is famous for its scenery is also
famous for its suicides." After one girl jumped into the Mihara Volcano,
over nine hundred followed in the same year. Many believed the legend
that they would be instantly cremated and sent to heaven in a beautiful
plume of smoke.

Nature and suicide are part of a Japanese tendency to romanticize
suicide. When it was rumored that a virgin killed herself in a love-pact
suicide, the purity of the suicide led to songs, poems, and movies. But if
Akutagawa's suicide note is any indication, romanticism may simply be

a culturally accepted disguise for less noble reasons for suicide. He dies disliking everything, including himself. A very unromantic notion.

Yukio Mishima

By the age of forty-five, the Japanese writer Yukio Mishima had done it all. He had produced thirty-three plays and twenty novels. He had directed and acted in his own movies. He had even mastered karate and traditional samurai sword fighting.

His fame as a writer came from his ability to articulate the troubles of a changing Japan. He brilliantly captured the conflict between the traditional and the modern, but could never reconcile the gulf between the two worlds. As he aged, he became nostalgic for the traditional Japan and turned to nationalism.

Like many on the right, Mishima felt humiliated by the surrender agreement of World War II. He was particularly hurt to see the once-proud Japanese army reduced to a small defense force called the Jieitai. Mishima became obsessed with the fate of the Jieitai and hoped to see them one day rise to restore Japan's once-proud military.

One of the steps on the road to suicide is obsession with seemingly small details. In this case, Mishima became obsessed with the fact that the government chose to use the police force instead of the Jieitai army to quell a political protest rally. Mishima had seen this as a perfect opportunity to amend the Peace Constitution and restore the army. The missed opportunity festered in Mishima's mind until it became all-encompassing.

On November 25, 1970, Mishima finished the last installment of his epic *The Sea of Fertility*. It had taken him six years. He then drove to an appointment he had with a general of the Jieitai. With a few followers, he kidnapped the general and forced him to assemble his soldiers. Mishima put on a traditional Samurai headband and began his final speech.

As part of the hostage agreement, Mishima had asked for complete silence. Instead, the soldiers kept up a constant barrage of heckling. Mishima had planned a dramatic exit speech. It turned into a humiliating spectacle.

The nation has no spiritual foundation. That is why you don't agree with me! You don't understand Japan. The Jieitai must put things right. . . . Listen . . . be quiet will you . . . Don't you hear . . . Just listen to me! What happened last year? On October 21? There was a demonstration, an antiwar demonstration. On October 21 last year. In Shinjuku. And the police put it down. The police! After that there was, and there will be, no chance to amend the Constitution.

Listen! Listen! Listen! Listen! A man appeals to you! A man! I am staking my life on this! Do you hear? Do you follow me? If you do not rise with me, if the Jieitai will not rise, the Constitution will never be amended! You will be just American mercenaries. American troops!

I have waited for four years! Yes, four years! I wanted the Jieitai to rise! Four years! I have come to the last thirty minutes. Yes, the last thirty minutes. I am waiting . . . Are you men? You are soldiers! Then why do you stand by the constitution? You back the constitution that denies your very existence.

Then you have no future! You will never be saved! It is the end. The Constitution will remain forever. You are finished. You are unconstitutional! Listen! You are unconstitutional. The Jieitai is unconstitutional! You are all unconstitutional! Don't you understand? Will any of you rise with me?

You will not rise. You will do nothing. The constitution means nothing to you. You are not interested. I have lost my dream of the Jieitai! I salute the emperor. Tenno Heika Banzai! Tenno Heika Banzai! Tenno Heika Banzai! [Long live the emperor!]

After Mishima finished his speech to the soldiers, he fled into the building telling his men his last words: "They did not hear me very well." It was then time for his final act, as described by Henry Scott-Stokes in the *Life and Death of Yukio Mishima:* First he took off his jacket, unlaced his boots, and knelt on the carpet. In his right hand, he calmly held a foot-long dagger, called a yoroidoshi. One of his soldiers came forward with a brush and a piece of paper for Mishima to write a last message with his blood, but he refused.

Mishima found a spot on his lower abdomen and placed the knife against the spot. He shouted, "Long live the emperor!" and then let out a wild shout to drive all the air from his body. He plunged the dagger into his body. His face went white and his hand began to tremble. He began to make a horizontal cut across his stomach. His hand shook violently. He brought his left hand to help. He continued cutting crosswise. Blood spurted from the cut.

One of his soldiers readied to deliver the final blow. He brought the sword crashing down—and missed, slashing Mishima on the back and shoulder. He struck again—and missed, creating another gaping wound. Mishima was on the ground, twisting from side to side, blood shooting from his neck. The third blow was on target, but not strong enough. Finally, another soldier stepped forward and finished the job, separating Mishima's head completely from his body. The room began to smell: Mishima's intestines were now lying on the ground.

Mishima had prepared all his life for his act of hari-kari. He had spent hours weight lifting so his body would be beautiful enough for the noble death. He even practiced the act while performing in his films. The training paid off. Mishima's incision was seventeen centimeters long, a length unparalleled in modern records of this ritual.

"In feudal times we believed that sincerity resided in our entrails, and if we needed to show our insincerity, we had to cut our bellies and take out our visible sincerity. And it was also the symbol of the will of the soldier, the samurai; everybody knew that this was the most painful way to die. And the reason they preferred to die in the most excruciating manner was that it proved the courage of the samurai."

—Yukio Mishima

The ancient act of hari-kari, called *seppuku* in Japan, was originally a form of protest suicide. Over time, it developed into an act reserved for the defeated or humiliated samurai warrior.

It is a painful death. First, the samurai plunges a sharp dagger into his stomach. Then he attempts to make a long incision. At the first sign of alteration of the traditional posture, an assistant waiting with a sword beheads the subject.

It is easy to dismiss Mishima's hari-kari as the act of a nationalist zealot. But he was too intelligent to be an ideologue. He couldn't possibly believe that he could overthrow the government or change even a minor facet of modern Japan. Instead, he meant his public act to be an artistic and political statement. He left a speech, a perfect body, and a warrior's death, all to remind those of what Japan once was. As he wrote to a friend: "After thinking and thinking through for years, I came to wish to sacrifice myself for the old, beautiful tradition of Japan, which is disappearing very quickly day by day."

Whether Mishima succeeded in his public gesture is another matter. Except for a few on the right wing, most thought him simply a madman. A book reviewer for *The New York Times* was less charitable. He failed to see the artistic or political gesture in the public suicide. Instead, he called Mishima "a sadomasochistic homosexual for whom death was the ultimate act of exhibitionism and self-gratification. It would not be too much to see Mr. Mishima's suicide as a fatal form of masturbation."

The countries with the highest suicide rates are Hungary, Finland, and Russia, which have rates twice as high as Japan. No one knows why Hungary heads the list. Dr. Ceza Varady, Director of the Institute for Mental Health in Budapest has suggested the "phenomenon reflects the Hungarian temperament, which is volatile and likes dramatic gestures." The Catholic countries of Italy and Ireland have relatively low suicide rates. Countries not only have different rates, but different methods of suicide. In ancient Greece, the preference was hemlock. In Rome, it was stabbing. In nineteenth-century Paris, drowning was popular, and fishermen were paid for every body they caught. In America, the gun is the choice, especially among men. American women tend to overdose on drugs, although they, too, are beginning to choose guns. In England, where there is strict gun control, the method of choice is gas. In Germany, it's hanging. Japan is of course known for hari-kari. Russians are famous for jumping in front of trains. This has literary roots in Tolstoy's heroine Anna Karenina. Today, the train may be a practical necessity. In Moscow, guns and drugs are expensive, rooftops are restricted, and the city has few bridges.

Russia

I am leaving this place forever,
without thoughts,
without hope,
without work,
alone in the dark of night.
The snow will cover my footsteps
A note left in the cold, dark exile of Siberia

While the Soviet Union kept no reliable suicide statistics, if the list of famous names is any indicator, Communism took a heavy toll on the psyche. A high rate of alcoholism added to the problem, but probably most difficult to deal with was the capricious nature of the rule. On the whim of anyone from Stalin to a petty bureaucrat, a person could be famous one day, in exile the next. Perhaps that's why even Stalin's wife chose suicide.

With the collapse of Communism, Russians are now killing themselves so often that the suicide rate is third in the world, after Hungary and Finland.

Vladimir Mayakovsky

Mayakovsky was a heralded poet of the Russian Revolution, but he soon fell from favor with the political establishment and found his works boycotted by the official writer's union. Mayakovsky took this rejection to heart, and at the age of thirty-six, he committed suicide.

To Everyone
    The fact that I die is no one's fault and, please, don't gossip. The deceased especially hate that.
    Mama, sisters and comrades, forgive me—it's not the best way (I don't recommend it to others), but I have no other exit.
    Lilia—love me.
    My Comrade Government, my family is Lilia Brik, my mother, my sisters, and Veronica Vitoldovna Polonskaya.
    If you can arrange a tolerable life for them—thanks.
    Give my poems in progress to the Brik family, they will take care of them.
As they say—
    "the final juicy incident is closed"
my beloved boat
    is broken on the rocks of daily life.
I've paid my debts
    and no longer need to count
pains I've suffered at the hands of others
    The misfortunes
        and the insults.
Good luck to those who remain
    Vladimir Mayakovsky.
P.S. Comrades, don't think me weak.

                                          Vladimir Mayakovsky
                                          4/12/30

Seriously—There's nothing to be done
  Hello.
Tell Ermilov that it's a pity I took down the slogan—
  should have cursed.

  In the desk I have 2,000 rubles—use it for taxes.
  Get the rest from the State Publishing House.

After his death, Stalin rehabilitated Mayakovsky, saying: "Mayakovsky was and remains the most talented poet of our Soviet epoch." Practically overnight, the boycotted poet became a hero of the revolution. Squares were named in his honor and statues erected.

12

The Right to Die

Have a nice trip.
Jack Kevorkian's words to Janet Adkins as she flipped the switch of his suicide machine. Her response: "Thank you."

Many psychologists believe that suicide by its very nature is an irrational act. Indeed, most of the notes so far show extreme disturbance. So, are the terminally ill actually the mentally ill?

As psychologist David Clark says, "The public has the notion that there's something different about elderly suicides—that it has a logic to it that others don't." We decry the skyrocketing adolescent suicide rate, but we fail to notice that the elderly rate is twice as high. We also fail to admit that older people can suffer from flawed judgment, impulsiveness, and mental illness. In fact, it is estimated that 50 percent of elderly suicides are the result of depression.

Some notes from elderly suicides do show the isolation and loneliness of depression, but many also show the heartbreaking pain and suffering of physical illness. These notes often evoke sympathy, and the suicide is accepted by society as understandable, even desired. But is the writer aware of this effect and deliberately crafting the note in a socially accepted manner? Is the note simply an attempt to disguise loneliness and depression, to make suicide palatable for all involved?

Complicating the matter is that many elderly and terminally ill attach themselves to the right to die movement, giving the act a political and public quality. Organizations like the Hemlock Society may provide advice, but they also provide comfort, company, and ultimately, meaning. One can die to escape pain and also for a greater cause. The suicide note then becomes a political statement, a manifesto for the right to die.

The notes that follow are documents far more complicated than one could ever predict. These reasoned, compelling notes may be political manifestos; they may be a socially accepted disguise of mental illness; or they may indeed be the terrible suffering of terminal illness. How we view these notes is not simply a matter of heuristics, it is a profound decision on whether suicide is ever rational.

The time is approaching when we shall consider it abhorrent to our civilization to allow a human being to die in prolonged agony which we should mercifully end in any other creature. Believing this choice to be of social service in promoting wiser views on this question, I have preferred Chloroform to cancer.

From the note of Charlotte Perkins Gilman, she was seventy-five years old.

Dear God,
Please have mercy on my soul. . . .
Please forgive me, I can't stand the pain anymore.

This seventy-six-year-old grandmother, isolated by depression and disability, crawled into her freezer and died.

I'm bored with my bodily functions and my mind is going. It's better to end it now while I can still do something.

A note from a fifty-two-year-old sufferer of multiple sclerosis. Her husband was sentenced to six months in jail for helping her commit suicide.

> *It is not decent for Society to make a man do this to himself. Probably, this is the last day I will be able to do it myself.*

This is from the suicide note of Nobel Prize–winning physicist Percy Bridgman, who, suffering from cancer, shot himself at the age of seventy-nine.

> *After three and one half years I find I can no longer go on with this pain and agony. I have not been out of the house in three years except to go to Detroit to see my doctor. I don't call this living. . . . I'm so glad there is a Dr. Kevorkian to help me. . . . If God won't come to me I'm going to go to God.*

Marjorie Wantz, aided in her suicide by Jack Kevorkian

The suicide rate increases with age and is highest for those over sixty-five. The elderly rate has risen twenty percent since 1980, and the use of guns, the most lethal and successful means, has gone up fifty-five percent. When the elderly attempt suicide, they usually succeed.

Studies of suicide notes show a clear difference with age. The notes of younger suicides show more hate both toward themselves and others, as well as more aggression. The notes of older suicides show more hopelessness, despair, and fatigue.

Psychologist Antoon Leenaars has characterized suicide notes by age:

20–39 preoccupied with relationships
40–49 unequal to demands of life
50–59 do not leave reasons, but instructions
60 +   illness, pain, loneliness, and isolation

Arthur and Cynthia Koestler

"There is only one prospect worse than being chained to an intolerable existence: the nightmare of a botched attempt to end it."

—Arthur Koestler

Philosopher and author Arthur Koestler was an active member of the British right to die group, Exit, even writing an essay for them entitled, "A Guide to Self Deliverance." At the age of seventy-seven, with his health deteriorating, he followed his own guide and chose self-deliverance. His wife, at fifty-five and in perfect health, joined him. They left a suicide note, excerpted below, the first part had been written by Koestler eight months earlier.

> . . . *My reasons for deciding to put an end to my life are simple and compelling: Parkinson's Disease and the slow-killing variety of leukemia (CCL) . . .*
>
> *I wish my friends to know that I am leaving their company in a peaceful frame of mind, with some timid hopes for a depersonalized after-life beyond due confines of space, time and matter and beyond the limits of our comprehension. This "oceanic feeling" has often sustained me at difficult moments, and does so now, while I am writing this.*
>
> *What makes it nevertheless hard to take this final step is the reflection of the pain it is bound to inflict on my few surviving friends, and above all my wife Cynthia . . .*

At the bottom of the note, Cynthia added:

> *I should have liked to finish my account of working for Arthur—a story which began when our paths happened to cross in 1949. However, I cannot live without Arthur, despite certain inner resources.*

Friends of Koestler's worried that he might have waited too long to commit suicide. In his last days he could barely talk, walk, or think straight.

These same friends were shocked by Cynthia's suicide. She was twenty years younger and in perfect health. Perhaps she had merged her life so completely with the man she loved that she could not live without him. Or perhaps she was emotionally coerced by a domineering husband. Suicide expert Edwin Shneidman thought the latter when he paraphrased Arthur's suicide note: "I'm going to kill myself, aren't we?"

Cynthia's suicide points out inherent dangers in the right to die movement. Clearly, the methods advocated by Exit, the Hemlock Society, and other groups are being used to assist not just the terminally ill like Arthur Koestler, but physically healthy people like Cynthia. Hemlock cofounder Ann Humphry's suicide (page 10) raises the same issue.

Many argue that to condone any suicide, no matter how rational, will send society careening down a slippery slope. The mentally ill might confuse their case with the terminally ill. The terminally ill might find that the right to die has become the duty to die, with the sick and the poor coerced into suicide for economics or convenience.

The Netherlands, known for its liberal but careful approach to euthanasia, is a case in point. Herbert Hendin, executive director of the American Suicide Foundation, criticizes the Dutch for involuntarily and indiscriminately assisting in suicide: "The Dutch Government's own commissioned research," he says, "has documented that in more than 1,000 cases a year, doctors actively caused or hastened death without the patient's request. Virtually every guideline established by the Dutch to regulate euthanasia has been modified or violated with impunity. A healthy but grief stricken social worker mourning the death of her son two months earlier was assisted in suicide. A man in his 30's who is HIV positive but who has no symptoms and may not develop them for years was also helped to die, without any effort to address the terror behind his desire to end his life. Euthanasia in the Netherlands—intended as an unfortunate necessity in exceptional cases—has become almost a routine way of dealing with serious or terminal illness, and even with grief."

Like many who are against active euthanasia, Hendin believes we, as a society, need instead to learn how to properly take care of the terminally ill, allowing them to die a pain-free and dignified, but natural death.

Ron Berst

To San Francisco Police Department—or equivalent Jurisdiction.

This is to state that I, Ron R. Berst (Mother's maiden name is Swinburne), did take my own life, due to the fact that I have the disease AIDS, and it has progressed both rapidly, and to the point where:

1) How ill I constantly feel and have almost no energy, and:

2) I very soon expect to become a burden to my friends and family, and I do not want to put any of them through such an ordeal.

Further, I want to be remembered as a fairly active, vibrant, caring, individual—how people perceive of me now, not the bedridden, sickly, forgetful person that I can see myself starting a path towards becoming . . .

I sincerely regret any inconvenience that this may have caused anyone involved. I honestly believe that a fast end such as this— while one is still able—yet ill enough to justify it, is easier on my close friends, who have been so unbelievably supportive emotionally for me, and my family, who have been no less so, than to drag this out.

I did NOT "give up."

With AIDS, as you know it is fairly downhill—without much (any) hope for a reversal. This way I am remembered the way I WANT to be remembered—and my friends can go on with their lives, and perhaps the dollars saved in not having to "drag my survival out to the end" can perhaps be better spent or applied to finding a cure for this disease, so my friends may not have to go through what I have.

Ron Berst jumped off the Golden Gate Bridge. In his will he donated $10,000 to AIDS research.

Ron Berst's note makes it clear he wants to take action while he still can. He had probably seen many of his friends with AIDS prepare for suicide, but then suffer AIDS dementia and become unable to perform the act. They cruelly suffered the fate they had hoped to avoid.

There are two camps in the AIDS community: those who believe in fighting the disease to the bitter end and see suicide as giving up; and those who feel they are fighting a losing battle, and see suicide as their only means of control over the disease. Berst is well aware of this debate and structures his note as a rationale for suicide. He makes that clear with his line: "I did NOT 'give up.'"

Berst's eloquent letter helps to explain why people with AIDS kill themselves at a rate up to twenty times higher than the general population. A complicating factor, though, is that both secondary infections and medications can cause suicidal depression. *The New York Times* describes the story of George K., an AIDS sufferer who was very sick, with a high fever and continual diarrhea. In despair, he called a friend and asked for help committing suicide. Luckily, his friend urged him to check into a hospital. Tests found a parasitic infection that could be treated. "I'd be dead no question," George says. "Even if I wasn't successful the first time, I would have kept trying because I was so miserable."

George though, like many AIDS sufferers, still sees suicide as the only way to gain control over the disease. He has now gathered the drugs he will need when the time comes. Having the means to kill myself "has made my everyday better, much much better. It has diminished my horror, as though I was facing my enemy on a battlefield stark naked and now I have armor."

Jo Roman

The right to die movement is usually concerned with terminal illness. But Jo Roman argues the radical view that healthy people should commit suicide as a way to bring ideal closure to their lives.

Her suicide note explains her philosophy of "rational suicide."

By the time you read these lines I WILL HAVE GENTLY ENDED my life on the date of this letter's postmark.

More than a decade ago I concluded that suicide need not be pathological. Further, that rational suicide makes possible a truly ideal closing of one's life span. Commitment to a rational suicide spares one erosive accelerating investment against unwanted existence.

More important by far than such practical avoidance, however, is the paradoxical life-enriching value of suicide. Life perspectives clouded by the vagaries and fears of open-endedness become crystal clear.

. . . I decided I would set an exit date and prepare to meet it. I'd aim for my exit date to predate discomfort of intensity which might diminish my chance of CREATING ON MY OWN TERMS THE FINAL STROKE OF MY LIFE'S CANVAS.

No treasure of my life—and there are many!—is greater than the growth emerging from the approach to my death.

I can say, however, that I believe time is at hand when consciousness of personal responsibility for the length of one's life span—as well as for its content—will establish RATIONAL SUICIDE AS A BASIC HUMAN RIGHT TO BE GIVEN SOCIETY'S ASSISTANCE AND PROTECTION.

The difference between killing oneself and bringing one's life to a responsible good end is the very real difference between pathological and rational suicide. I urge each of you to begin as early as possible—

I HOPE YOU WILL WORK TO SHAPE YOUR OWN LIFE AND TO CREATE A GOOD END TO DIGNIFY IT. THEN, LET PEACE WASH OVER YOU TOO!

Jo Roman hopes one day for an "Exit House," a lush suicide hotel complete with swimming pool, library, and garden. This might comfort the many elderly who do not want to die alone.

Dying alone seems to be a fear of all suicides. The elderly prevent it by linking themselves to groups like the Hemlock Society. Other suicides seek company by choosing public places or famous suicide spots. In the end, isn't the last desperate communication of a suicide note a way of contact and connecting, a way ultimately to prevent dying alone?

Acknowledgments

I would like to thank those who believed in the idea and helped turn it into reality—namely, my editors at Riverhead, Kathryn Crosby and Nicholas Weinstock, and my agents at Palmer and Dodge, Nicholas Audy-Rowland, Jill Kneerim, and Lane Zachary. For legal review, I would like to thank Gina Anderson and Mark Fischer. And of course thanks to all those who helped throughout including Heather Ainsworth, Kirk Barton, David Berenson, Carla Berst, Joseph Blatt, Cindy Bond, Colin Brady, Joan Branham, the Chedd-Angier Production Company, George Howe Colt, Kay Council, Kenny Dinkin, Nancy Dubuc, Joanna Epstein, Gary Glassman, Mamor Iga, David Irving, Ken Kesey, Cathy Koerwer, Matt Kursh, Antoon Leenaars, Richard Lewis, Nancy Lipsitz, Marti Louw, David McKillop, Barbara Moran, Michelle Oishi, Thomas Ott, Pinball Productions, Cindy Powell, Laura Russell, Chris Schmidt, Edwin Shneidman, and Craig Wilkey.

All of the notes in this book have been previously published. The sources for each chapter follows:

Chapter 1: The Birth of The Suicide Note

Suicide notes in this chapter were found in *Sleepless Souls: Suicide in Early Modern England* by Michael MacDonald and Terence Murphy; *Victorian Suicide: Mad Crimes and Sad Histories* by Barbara Gates; *Suicide in Victorian and Edwardian England* by Olive Anderson; and *The Gentleman's Magazine* Vol's XIII (1743), XX (1750) and XL (1770). Leenaars quote from *Suicide Notes* by Antoon Leenaars.

Chapter 2: Love and Hate

The A. Alvarez quote (as are all his quotes in this book) is from *The Savage God*. This chapter includes notes and biographical information from Edwin Shneidman's *Voices of Death*; Jacques Choron's *Suicide*; Howard Wolf's article "Suicide Notes" in *The American Mercury,* November 31, 1931; and Edward Robb Ellis and George Allen's *The Traitor Within: Our Suicide Problem*. Marx's note originally appeared in Yvonne Kapp's *Eleanor Marx*. Boulanger's note appeared in *Le General Boulanger* by Fresnette Pisani-Ferry and was translated by Joan Branham. The excerpt from Humphry's note and videotape as well as the biographical information appeared in *The New York Times Magazine,* December 8, 1991.

Chapter 3: To the Point

Suicide notes in this chapter were found in Ellis and Allen's *The Traitor Within*; George Howe Colt's *The Enigma of Suicide*; Dublin and Bunzel's *To Be or Not To Be*; Glen Evans's *The Encyclopedia of Suicide,*

Cleveland Plain Dealer January 29, 1985 and *New York* magazine, September 27, 1982. Howard Wolf's "Suicide Notes" in *The American Mercury,* November 31, 1931.

Chapter 4: Disgrace
Henry's note appeared in Jean-Denis Bredin's *The Affair: The Case of Alfred Dreyfus* and translated by Jeffrey Mehlman. Charles Stuart's note appeared in the *Boston Herald,* February 1, 1993. Kammerer's note originally appeared in Neve Freie Presse, Vienna, September 25, 1926. Stephen Ward's note appeared in Philip Knightley and Caroline Kennedy's *An Affair of State: The Profumo Case and The Framing of Stephen Ward.* Hitler's note appeared in *The Life and Death of Adolf Hitler* by Robert Payne. Göring's notes appeared in *Göring: A Biography* by David Irving. Simpson's note was read at a news conference on June 17, 1994. Genius's note appeared in *The Traitor Within* by Ellis and Allen. Godwin's note and Shneidman's quote from *Voices of Death* by Edwin Shneidman. Beddoes' note from *Thomas Lovell Beddoes: An Anthology,* edited by F. L. Lucas. Ruth R.'s note appeared in "Suicide Notes" by Howard Wolf, *The American Mercury,* November 31, 1931.

Chapter 5: Altruistic Suicide
The brief notes in this chapter originally appeared in *Separate Paths: Why People End Their Lives* by Linnea Pearson with Ruth Purtilo; *Craig and Joan* by Eliot Asinof, "Suicide Notes" by Howard Wolf, *The American Mercury,* November 31, 1931, as well as *The New York Times, Washington Post, The Observer, Los Angeles Times,* and *Charleston Gazette.* Additional quotes from A. Alvarez's *The Savage God* and Edwin Shneidman's *Voices of Death.*

Chapter 6: The Artistic Temperament

Van Gogh's note appeared in *The Collected Letters of Vincent Van Gogh.* Esenin's poem appeared in *Esenin: A Life* by Gordon McVay. Esenin's poem translated by Chris Schmidt. Pascin's note appeared in *Pascin* by Gaston Diehl. Woolf's note appeared in *Virginia Woolf: A Biography* by Quentin Bell. Cobain's note is from Courtney Love's memorial reading, printed in *Rolling Stone,* June 2, 1994. Kleist's note appeared in *Kleist: A Biography* by Joachim Maass and translated by Ralph Manheim. Kosinki excerpt from *Jerzy Kosinski: A Biography* by James Sloan Park. Celan quote from *Paul Celan: Poet, Survivor, Jew* by John Felstiner. Barton's note appeared in *The New York Times,* May 21, 1931. Parker's "Résumé" appeared in *The Poetry and Short Stories of Dorothy Parker.* Her note appeared in *Dorothy Parker: What Fresh Hell Is This?* by Marion Meade. The author wishes to thank the National Association for the Advancement of Colored People for authorizing the use of Dorothy Parker's work.

Various quotes from A. Alvarez's *The Savage God*; Loren Coleman's *Suicide Clusters; Boston Globe,* April 3, 1994; and *The New York Times,* April 27, 1981.

Chapter 7: In Public

Bud Dwyer's letter and the biographical information appeared in the *Philadelphia Inquirer,* January 23, 1987. The story of Christine C. appeared in *The New York Times,* July 16, 1974. Golden Gate notes were gathered from the *Los Angeles Times, Baltimore Sun, Washington Post* and Allen Brown's *Golden Gate: Biography of a Bridge.* Vince Foster's note was published in *The New York Times,* August 11, 1993. William Sytron's quote appeared in *Newsweek,* April 8, 1994.

Chapter 8: Hollywood Endings

This chapter was based on Kenneth Anger's *Hollywood Babylon* and *Hollywood Babylon II,* and Laurie Jacobson's *Hollywood Heartbreak.*

Chapter 9: Suicide Diaries

Pavese entries from *The Burning Brand: Diaries 1935–1950* translated by A. E. Murch. Haydon's journal from *The Autobiography and Memoirs of Benjamin Robert Haydon.* Oswald, Halliwell and Thomas Mallon quotes from *A Book of One's Own: People and Their Diaries* by Thomas Mallon. Arbus entry from *Diane Arbus: A Biography* by Patricia Bosworth. Massachusetts man, British physician, spider bite and chemist notes from *Traitor Within* by Ellis and Allen. Information on the psychological meaning of suicide methods is from George Howe Colt's *The Enigma of Suicide.*

Chapter 10: Mass Suicide

The final speech of Jim Jones was printed in *The New York Times,* March 15, 1979. Additional notes were printed in *The New York Times,* November 28, 1978 and December 18, 1978.

Chapter 11: Around the World

This chapter is based on Maroru Iga's book on suicide in Japan, *The Thorn in the Chrysanthemum.* The description of Mishima's hari-kari and the excerpt of his last speech appeared in *The Life and Death of Yukio Mishima* by Henry Scott-Stokes. The note from Siberia appeared in *The New York Times,* September 3, 1994. Mayakovsky's biographical information is from *I Love: The Story of Vladimir Mayakovsky and Lili Brik* by Ann and Samuel Charters. Mayakovsky's note translated by

Chris Schmidt. Vardy's quote appeared in Glen Evans's *Encyclopedia of Suicide*. Additional quotes and background on Japanese suicide from George Howe Colt's *Enigma of Suicide*.

Chapter 12: The Right to Die
Wantz's note appeared in the *Los Angeles Times,* November 25, 1991. Gilman's note appeared in *The New York Times,* August 20, 1935. Bridgman's note quoted from Sherwin Nuland's *How We Die.* Koestler's note from George Mikes's *Arthur Koestler: The Story of a Friendship.* Berst's note from the *San Francisco Examiner,* June 28, 1991. Roman's note from Exit House by Jo Roman. Hendin's quote from *The New York Times,* December 16, 1994. Other short notes and quotes from George Howe Colt's *Enigma of Suicide,* the *Boston Globe, The New Yorker,* and *The New York Times.*

Except for a handful of coroners and psychologists, **Marc Etkind** has probably read more suicide notes than anyone else. This he does for enjoyment. To actually earn a living, he writes, produces and directs television programs for Public Television and the Discovery Channel.